HOMELANDS

—— A MEMOIR ——

NEAL MOORE

TUSKER
PRESS

TUSKER PRESS
Suite 8, Private Bag X3
Roggebaai, 8012, South Africa

Copyright © Neal Moore 2013, 2017
All Rights Reserved.

A portion of "Homelands" was originally published
in Der Spiegel under the title "Ich fühlte mich
Mandela nahe"/"I felt close to Mandela" in 2013.

Neal Moore asserts the moral right to be identified
as the author of this work.

Cover & interior design: Zarina Rose Lagman.

ISBN 978-0-9985395-2-2

HOMELANDS

— A MEMOIR —

For the Sixishe Family:
A tribute to the transformation, reconciliation
and national unity of South Africa.

—N.M.

TABLE OF CONTENTS

PROLOGUE

On August 4, 1992, a march was called on Bisho, "capital" of the Ciskei, one of South Africa's puppet Bantustans, for a showdown with the puppet masters. It was called a puppet regime because the international community, along with most inhabitants of the Ciskei, never did recognize "Bantustans" as sovereign nations. They viewed these "homelands" for black South Africans as part and parcel of apartheid and the Ciskei honcho, Brigadier Joshua Gqozo, as a malevolent tool who must be toppled.

The march was spearheaded by the African National Congress with the stated purpose of ousting Gqozo by occupying Bisho. The fall of the Ciskei, the march organizers reasoned, could create a domino effect, leading to the collapse of other "homelands" and, eventually, the demise of the white-minority regime in Pretoria.

Missionaries of the Church of Jesus Christ of Latter-day Saints, who were operating in the Ciskei at the time, were caught off guard. We didn't comprehend the nuances of the politics, or the danger. Referred to as "elders" of our church, and so said the shiny black badges on our shirt pockets, most of us were still in our teens –

over-zealous, all-knowing and extraordinarily naïve.

Our sources were telling us on the morning of the "mass action" that, after the march from the Victoria cricket ground in King William's Town to Bisho, the crowd would march back to King William's Town and burn it to the ground.

That was the chatter all about us in Mdantsane township, on the telephone, from our neighbors, from the leaders of our church in the township – all in one spectacular volley of urgent messages. While the idea sounds sensational in retrospect, at the time, we could only believe what we heard and what we saw. For take one look out the windows of our pink little house in Mdantsane and hundreds of protesters were on the move, filing into minivan taxis, marching on foot, stirring up dust as they strode along while chanting slogans of *Umkhonto we Sizwe* (Spear of the Nation), their placards held high.

As outsiders set down in an unfamiliar land, we would sometimes experience what we referred to as "get the hell out of Dodge days," or "stay away days," when we would decamp to East London, an Indian Ocean port city in the Eastern Cape region. Everything would be going just dandy in Mdantsane, but then something would happen, some incident that would turn the mood of the township sour, and dangerous.

At such times, I would think of a nun who had been killed in the area in 1952. Although she had died four decades previous, she was always at the back of my mind, my only gauge regarding the safety of a white person in a black township, the only other white besides my missionary companions who understood our position, our place in the world. Early on during my assignment in Mdantsane, I asked an older resident of the township about the nun.

"Her name was Sister Quinlan and she was Irish," said Maureen Magwaca as she sat across the table from me during one of our weekly lessons in Xhosa, the language of the Xhosa people who inhabited the Ciskei. Maureen was a friend, a mother figure who I looked up to and loved with the entirety of my heart.

She'd stood up to the struggle in her own way, along with her family, and knew a hell of a lot about politics, language, and the human condition. She was one of my personal sources, a confidant who could help me make a semblance of sense out of the topic of life, and death. She reached across the table to hold onto my hands, a sweet gesture to ease my apprehensions, as she told me what happened.

"She didn't live in Mdantsane, but volunteered in Duncan Village, just outside," Maureen said of Sister Elsie Quinlan, of the Dominican order. "A law had just been passed that said blacks weren't allowed to gather outdoors, out in the open air, and there was a big protest. There was a mob and the mob was angry and she came in to help, and they attacked her."

"Is it true," I asked, "that the people had beaten her, had stoned her, had burned her, and had eaten her?"

"Yes, Neal, it is true. Some of the mob thought they could take her power by tearing into her flesh, but what you should know is there were others who tried to stop it, who tried to save her."

"I believe it," I said.

Sister Quinlan had been working with the Xhosa, as we were doing. And, like us, she had become too confident, too trusting.

I don't know quite how to describe our feelings while living and working in the township. I imagined, perhaps naively, that I and my fellow missionaries were surrounded by a bubble of safety. I knew we were living in what, essentially, was a war zone as South Africa's blacks fought for emancipation from white-minority rule. But because of the work we were doing, because of our intense emotional attachment to the people we served, and our belief that the feeling was mutual, I felt protected. I felt, most of the time, that I'd be just fine. I supposed that Sister Quinlan felt the same.

So when we were warned that it would be prudent to pack up and stay away for a few days, just to be on the safe side, we didn't think twice. We understood, if only because of Sister Quinlan's grisly fate, that when the tide shifted, we had to clear out.

On this particular morning, the shift occurred with such

velocity that we almost didn't make it. Living and working on foot in the depths of the township, by day and night for months at a time, I felt in an odd sort of way that my ethnicity didn't matter, as though I had somehow transcended the race barrier that divided South Africa at that time, divided my home community in Los Angeles, and divided the history of my church. But when the shit hit the fan, and it happened many times during my time in Mdantsane, I'd take a long look at myself in the bathroom mirror at our home, light a joint to mellow out, take a few drags, and feel extraordinarily exposed, extraordinarily white.

The longer we waited on this particular morning, the more exposed we felt. The highway to the west between Mdantsane and King William's Town was definitely a no-go as protesters were reportedly on the move along the road. Our dilemma: Do we stay and risk death in the township or take our chances on the highway between Mdantsane and East London? The decision was up to the branch president, the leader of our church in the township, a kindly Xhosa man who worked as a detective for the Ciskei police. He talked to his own sources and confirmed that, with a little luck, the road to East London should be passable.

We hastily grabbed our bags and loaded up our lightning blue Corolla as an unspoken fear invaded our minds. *We just might not make it; that safety bubble had burst.* I could smell that fear among the elders that day as we hightailed it along the main back road of the township, no one saying a word. It was one of those drives where you sit quite rigid in your seat, white knuckled with fists out in front, to steady you, to protect you, to will your journey well. We slowed down in spots where protesters were using the same stretch of road to get to the highway. At one point, marchers surrounded our car, rocked it back and forth and pounded on the windows. The oversized church magnets on either side of the car were not doing the trick. There were too many people now pushing up against us and all the crowd could see was the enemy, their eyes dancing about wildly, angrily focusing on a car full of whites. We accelerated through the crowd and eventually made it to the motorway between King William's Town and East London. As the Corolla pointed toward East London, all four of us breathed a sigh of relief.

Moments after turning onto the highway, we witnessed a convoy of South African Defence Force Casspirs, gargantuan, landmine-protected vehicles of death, carrying armed soldiers toward King William's Town, presumably to protect the city from the protesters after their march on Bisho. I brought my camera up to the window to snap a photo, an action that, I was told later, could have landed us in jail.

The motorway in the direction of King William's Town was heavily congested with foot traffic and minivans. The ratio of protesters to Casspirs was overwhelmingly in favor of the protesters.

As a result, our fellow missionaries based in King William's Town didn't get out in time. King William's Town, like many of South Africa's dorps, or small towns, was then mainly white. It was just outside the borders of the Ciskei and was only a short distance from the black townships inside the Bantustan, sprawling tracts of spartan government-built housing that provided labor for white families. Arriving from all directions, protesters were marching on the stadium on Old Maitland Road between King William's Town and Bisho. Two fellow missionaries trapped in King William's Town holed up with the white leader of the Mormon Church in the town, along with his family, who happened to be nudists. Armed with little more than semiautomatic weapons, the family barricaded the doors of their colonial bungalow and pointed their guns out the windows toward the street.

I talked later to one of these missionaries, who told me in confidence, on the verge of tears and still trying to shake off the terror, that he never thought he'd end up cradling a shotgun on his mission and that he had shaken himself silly with fear. Fear, of course, for his personal safety, but also fear that, if the situation would have gone south, he might have been forced to pull the trigger.

As things turned out, the demonstration in nearby Bisho ended with soldiers of the Ciskei Defence Force firing their weapons into the sand between themselves and the protesters, serving as a precursor for a much larger and deadlier demonstration a month later. That "mass action" on September 7 would attract about eighty thousand demonstrators and result in the deaths of twenty-eight marchers and one soldier of the Ciskei Defence Force. It would become known as the Bisho Massacre.

The four of us who had fled the August demonstration made it to East London, where we spent three or four days until it was deemed safe enough to head back to Mdantsane, to take up residence again in our little house in NU 17, or, Native Unit 17.

But now things were different. No longer did we have that jovial, carefree feeling that we'd experienced before the August 4 march. Tensions had been ratcheted up, and it was palpable. Folks didn't smile so readily as before. They walked briskly about their business, not looking up and no longer shaking hands.

For the first time I realized why so few houses in the township bore painted addresses, especially in our neighborhood, where some residents were soldiers, town councilmen, or otherwise considered collaborators with Brigadier Gqozo's military government in Bisho. Those who were employed by the state, who had stood on the wrong side of that sand at Bisho, were persona non grata. Entire families of government employees abandoned their houses in the township to take up residence in a tent city rumored to have sprung up within the walls of the brigadier's military base, and even at his personal farm, Blacklands. Those connected to Gqozo's regime who remained in the township, who hadn't marched on Bisho, were quite simply fucked, subject to the threat of reprisal killings, often carried out in the name of the ANC.

Just after our return, a trio of children took our hands and led us to a burned-out house, not far from our own. They told us that the community wanted the policeman who lived there to explain why he supported Gqozo. No one responded to knocks on the door. So, amid taunting and chanting, the children told us, the house was surrounded and set alight. As the man of the house emerged, along with his family, amid the fire and smoke, the mob had a tire waiting for him. And, thus, the "necklacing" began.

The children showed us the aftermath of what had transpired, pointing to a trail of scorched earth where the tire had passed. The policeman had been doused with petrol and the tire thrust over his head and about his torso. He was then rolled through the street in a whirling ball of flame and thick black smoke. The children told us that boys, just like them, had propelled the tire along on its deadly mission, jabbing the policeman and the tire with sticks to keep the tire rolling as the man burned. All the while, a taunting mob followed the tire's erratic course as the public execution turned into a feeding frenzy. Awash with power, at least for that moment, township residents found an outlet for their frustration and grasped the concept of freedom. Freedom from the stooge in Bisho and from his minions, and, by extension, freedom from South Africa's governing National Party, whose system of apartheid kept the country's blacks in a state of subjugation. The death of this policeman, at the swift, collective hands of a people's court, was a proxy blow against the white-minority government.

* * *

It was in this context of time and place and uneasiness of the mind that, not too long afterwards, as we were still coming to grips with the changed atmosphere in Mdantsane, we heard a knock on our back door, the one we generally used to come and go. Upon opening the door, we were greeted by four black men in dark suits, who introduced themselves as the "NU 17 Housing Committee." They asked if we'd be kind enough to join them for a meeting at their house, two doors down our street, later that night.

The men didn't smile as they spoke. And, besides their words, their suits told us they meant business. It was hard to refuse the meeting, but it was also hard not to sense trouble.

We called ahead to the local leader of our church, a black police detective by the name of Ndzaba, who had acted as our eyes and ears regarding "stay away" days, letting us know when followers of the African National Congress, or the more hard line Pan African Congress were going to hold demonstrations, of when it was or wasn't safe for us to stay. He said that this group was not a "housing committee" but rather local members of the ANC and that we'd be walking into an interrogation. We asked if we were in danger, and he answered by telling us he'd come with us, to help translate, if necessary, but really to make sure we'd be OK. Under his breath, he told us not to worry, that he'd be armed.

To prepare for that meeting, we shined our shoes and brushed our teeth and practiced our big-on-innocence smiles. At the appointed time, our church leader joined us and together we walked down the street to the meeting with the "housing committee."

The house was like any other except no family was present. Just a front room with sofas and chairs and five or six suit-clad men and one woman. They directed us inside and commanded us to sit. They took their places all around us, some standing and some sitting. The woman, with a notepad and pen, sat in a corner, scribbling down everything that was said.

Once we were seated, a thin man introduced the group as the "NU 17 Housing Committee" and said that they had some questions for us, that they wanted to get to know us better, to become better acquainted.

He feigned friendliness, but the expressions of the others in the room told us otherwise. Once he had made his introductory speech and sat down himself, he turned the floor over to a big, powerfully built man, who in his dark suit looked like a bouncer in a township *shebeen*. He had no time for pleasantries. He was after facts.

"What are your names and titles?" he asked brusquely.

"Elder Moore."

"Elder Basjan."

"Elder Greenhorn."

"Elder Black."

"Which country do you come from?"

"America," chimed three of us.

"South Africa," said Basjan.

"How long have you lived here – in Mdantsane?"

"We've all been here for different amounts of time," I explained. "But I've been here the longest, for six months."

"How many in your group, how many of you white *umfundisi* from America?" he asked, using a Xhosa term of respect for a learned person.

"Four, at any given time."

"No, what I mean to say is, how many in your group? How many followers do you have? How many in your church?"

"Thirty-seven, inside Mdantsane."

"And what is your purpose, may I ask? What is it that you do?"

"We knock on doors and greet people. We volunteer at the hospital, Cecilia Makiwane. We dig in people's back yards and help them with their gardens, with their vegetables. We pick up trash, the plastic bags that blow all about and stick to the thorn bushes and trees."

"You do realize you are the only whites who live here?"

"Yes, we have noticed that."

Then followed a volley of additional questions that must have lasted thirty or so minutes, many of the questions trivial, as if on purpose, setting us up for what really mattered. For in time we came to the meat and potatoes of the questions, the crux of the discussion, if you will, the question the group here assembled had been itching to ask from the start, being the question they had clearly saved for last – the only question that really mattered.

The bruiser took a seat as he handed the floor over to a different man, to the most senior member of the group, sitting off to the side, who had been silently observing while scratching his chin. Clad in a suit a shade darker than the others, he now wiped his brow as he took a deep breath, delivering his question as more of a statement, his face angry and at the same time apprehensive. There was a pause as the lady in the corner looked up in an effort to write down the question and our statement correctly. And then the man in the dark suit spoke.

"What we want to know is," said the man, "are you now or have you ever been associated with the American CIA?"

Rule No. 53: Do not handle firearms.
Rule No. 100: Do not get involved in politics.
Rule No. 102: Do not give any information about the area.

The four of us missionaries looked at each other as the gravity of the situation sank in. The local leadership of the ANC thought we were American spies. Why else would a trio of young white Americans take up residence in a place like Mdantsane?

We wanted to answer the questions honestly and to help our neighbors understand. But we also wanted to walk out of the meeting. I glanced at our friend, the detective, and the man in the dark suit followed my glance, as if he knew that Detective Ndzaba was armed with a police service revolver.

I began to sweat, not unlike the man asking us questions, our questioner, as the random fact flew across my mind that Mormons are disproportionately represented in the U.S. State Department, FBI and CIA, thanks in great part to their overseas experience in situations just like ours. And I felt guilty and I felt scared as I realized it didn't matter how we responded, that the group would make their own judgment, a look of guilt written all over my bright and shiny face. *Mormon missionaries*, I considered, looking over to my compatriots, who sat nervously clasping onto their scriptures, busily studying their respective shoes on the floor. Gallivanting ourselves into the far flung reaches of the world's hot spots, white shirts and dark ties and *The Book of Mormon* in hand.

We said that, No, we were not connected to the CIA, that we were too young to be CIA – that there was no way the agency could employ teenagers. And the man in the dark suit grunted. And looked to his comrades, as they shook their heads, and stood to confer. In the end, after what felt like a bloody eternity of whispers, the lot turned back to us and nodded their heads, as if to signify they were finally satisfied.

As we stood and made our way to the door, I couldn't help but think to myself, of course. Had we been real spies, like my namesake, Uncle Neal, this would be the perfect cover – a cover that would have made my uncle proud. His cover having been a "telephone repairman" for General Electric while operating incognito for the CIA in Vietnam, Laos, and Cambodia during the height of the Vietnam War.

Outside, we took deep, appreciative breaths, happy for our freedom. We shook Detective Ndzaba's hand and thanked him for having our backs. We then turned and walked along the dusty path to our house, only a few paces away from an epicenter of danger, far too close for my liking.

HOMELAND
OF MIND

TOUCHDOWN

CHAPTER ONE

From the United States, it took us three and a half days to reach South Africa. During the last week of October 1991, we flew from Salt Lake City to Chicago's O'Hare and from O'Hare to Heathrow in London. After killing a day in London with a tour of Windsor Castle and a mad dash for fish and chips, we boarded a South African Airways Boeing 747-400 jumbo jet for an 11-hour, 5,639-mile night flight, down almost the entire length of the African continent to Johannesburg.

In the 1980s, international sanctions against apartheid had prevented South African Airways from flying across black Africa. Instead, SAA flights followed a wide arc around the western bulge of the continent, adding about three hours to the flight time and requiring refueling in such places as Lisbon, Gran Canaria Island and Ilha do Sal in the Cape Verde Islands. But in the late 1980s and early 1990s, the apartheid system began to crumble under the weight of the sanctions imposed from abroad and increasing militancy among the black majority at home. In 1991, President

F.W. de Klerk repealed the last of the apartheid laws, international sanctions were lifted and South African Airways was able to fly through the airspace of black African nations.

Our own flight through the African night had been uneventful but it afforded a bit of drama at the end. As we were on our final approach to Joburg's Jan Smuts International Airport, the captain announced on the cabin intercom that we were about to experience a hard landing and that we should assume the brace position – bent over, head between knees, hands over head, braced against the seat in front. The aircraft had apparently lost power in two of its four Rolls Royce engines, engines number three and four on the same side of the plane. "Not to worry," I recall the captain saying, as if we should consider ourselves lucky. "This airplane is more than capable of landing with only one engine, and we have two. But it's going to be a very rough landing. And so we have to *Brace! Brace! Brace!* – Brace now! Head between your legs! *Brace!*"

I'd been awake throughout the flight chatting up a fellow traveler, one of the female missionaries to whom I had taken a fancy, that I had just about fallen over the first time we had met. We'd been talking the entire night through to the point where our voices were raw. And at the exact moment I'd screwed up my courage to kiss her, the captain had begun screaming his urgent instructions, *Brace, Brace!* I looked up after instinctively ducking down and one steward who apparently hadn't heeded the captain's warning took flight across the galley as the giant 747 smacked down hard on the runway. I grabbed the girl as the plane bounced back up and then came down hard again for a second touchdown. But this time we were truly on terra firma, breathing deeply with an awkward, overt sigh of relief, rolling forward in the South African dawn.

I glanced out the window and across the runway, taking in the brilliant reds and browns of the scrub brush, dust and tawny grass in the day's first light. In my mind's eye, I also fancied that zebras and giraffes and maybe lions were out there in the bush going about their early-morning business. And here I was, like Dr. Livingstone before me, a white missionary in Africa.

* * *

I had only *just* been deemed worthy to become a missionary. It was a close call.

The honor of being selected for a mission is a defining moment in the life of a Mormon male, when he sheds the follies of youth in exchange for selfless service, with the bonus of seeing a bit of the world and becoming an "elder," a man. But I had some baggage: I had dabbled in drugs in high school and even did a bit of dealing to help finance the habit. And I wasn't a virgin, although I didn't disclose that to the church.

In case you're not aware, the Mormon Church has a rigid set of standards on who can join, who can serve and who is among the righteous, with a "temple recommend" – authorization to enter the House of the Lord – the ultimate talisman. I don't say that's all bad; it was just not for me. But life is a balancing act. I would take the bits that *were* for me and I'd run with them, like coming to Africa and pleasing my mom, shrugging my shoulders and shelving the rest.

What persuaded the church to allow me to serve as one of "God's soldiers" was that my stint as a drug-addled teenager hadn't been caused by rebellion and teen angst, but a desire to die – leading to a cocaine overdose at age fifteen. I'd lost my only brother, my hero, in an auto accident the year before and was having trouble coping without him. But I always had the love and support of my mother, who would hold my hand, sing Gaelic lullabies from her native Scotland and tell me that everything would be OK, although she was not well herself.

My mother was a convert to the LDS Church, and she was imbued with the zeal of a convert. My father had been born into the church, a "son of Utah Pioneers," as male Mormons with a long history in the church were called. But he had become "less active" – as he put it – until I was eight, when we moved to a house two blocks from the Los Angeles Temple on Santa Monica Boulevard in the Westwood neighborhood of West LA. An imposing edifice faced with white stone, the temple has a spire that soars 257 feet into the air, topped by a 15-foot gilded statue of the angel Moroni that glinted in the California sun. Perhaps because we lived, literally, in the shadow of the temple, the center of Mormonism in Southern California, my father felt guilty that he hadn't been raising his sons in the faith. So we started going to church and my mother followed. She adopted the faith and became the most devout of all of us.

I am a sixth-generation Mormon. My great-, great-, great-grandfather, Henry William Miller, was an early pioneer in the LDS church. He founded a settlement that became Council Bluffs, Iowa, served a mission to the Cherokee Nation and led the Henry W. Miller Handcart Company two hundred and twenty-nine pioneers and sixty-three wagons across the West toward the promised land, what Brigham Young called Zion, Salt Lake City. Miller had been friends with Orrin Porter Rockwell, known in legend as the "Destroying Angel of Mormondom," and was among the first white settlers in the Arizona Territory. Henry William Miller was a trailblazer, a tough guy, and if you go today to Council Bluffs, a picturesque town perched on the banks of the Missouri River, you'll find a statue of my heavy-bearded forbearer, a Book of Mormon in his left hand and an ax in the right.

With these genes swimming about in my bloodstream, I don't know if I can ever say that I'm no longer a Mormon. I don't go to church so I would be considered non-practicing. I'm not against the church, you understand, but I'm definitely not for it. The truth is I'm reluctant to say that my ancestors were wrong that Henry William Miller was a fool, that leading folks along the Mormon Trail was a folly, that my mother taking up the faith was a fluke. I was barely a practicing Mormon on my mission and I am non-practicing today. But you can never really get away from the faith, even if you wanted to.

My mother was my guiding light, and I tried to be strong for her throughout my teen years. But it hadn't been easy; I had stumbled more than she knew. I saw a mission as a tribute to her, a chance for redemption. My acceptance for a mission had been her fervent wish. She'd hold my hand, look into my eyes and tell me she wanted me to be a missionary. She wanted me to transform myself into something pure, and when I said goodbye shortly before heading for Africa, I realized that I'd probably never see her again.

* * *

I was born and grew up in Los Angeles. So at this point I must offer a disclaimer: a California Mormon is a different animal from a Utah Mormon. Different values. Different worldview. Different number of children in the family. Not so uptight and pious. More tolerant of those not of the faith. A different scenario all the way around.

In the early 1990s, it took six months to obtain a visa to enter South Africa. I saw the wait, in my hometown, as an opportunity to spend one last summer with my mother, who often told me how pleased she was that I was about to fulfill her wish.

Together, we had opened the letter from the church prophet: "Neal Moore, you are hereby called to serve for a period of twenty-four months in the South Africa Cape Town Mission." And every single day of that summer of 1991 as we'd spread out the *Los Angeles Times* on the breakfast table, photos of Nelson Mandela and F.W. de Klerk, of rioters and armored personnel carriers and smoke would greet us with their presence, would engulf my mind and my heart and my dreams; Mandela with a smile, de Klerk with a grimace.

Mandela had been released February 11, 1990, after twenty-seven and a half years of imprisonment, and the African National Congress was on the move. But not only the ANC. Every major political party – and there were apparently quite a few, most with military wings – was jockeying for power in the South Africa that would emerge from the turmoil. But, at this stage, I knew very little of the situation on the ground. All I knew was from the accounts in the *Los Angeles Times*, most of them swirling exclusively around the ANC.

I took a drive to see a friend from my high school days, then a student at the University of Southern California. Shannon White, still high from the previous night's revelry, was decked out in a disheveled toga crafted from a bed sheet when I visited his dorm room. My boyhood friend was very much with it, complete with a poster of Nelson Mandela up on his wall, right next to a ganja-wreathed Bob Marley.

We rolled a joint to ponder deep thoughts and once we'd struck a match and settled down to consider and ponder, Shannon blurted out, taking me by surprise: "Neal, I've talked it over with my parents and with our friends and we've decided you can't go to South Africa. We won't let you. The situation is just too dangerous."

I coughed, taken a bit aback, as if to consider. And when I said in a burst of youthful bravado, "I'm going, danger be damned," and he saw that I was serious, he nodded in agreement. His bluff was realized and I was saddened that he hadn't put on a bit more of a show, that he hadn't tried harder to persuade me not to go.

He asked what I thought of the situation in South Africa, of what I was about to hurl myself into, of where I was about to go. That, and if I thought he was a poser on account of his Mandela poster, readily admitting between intakes of his marijuana cigarette, "I have no idea what the man stands for, of what's going on."

"I have no idea, either," I said. "I have to go and experience it for myself, to dive right into the country with eyes wide open, and then I will hopefully understand."

* * *

The history of Mormon missionaries in South Africa was fraught with peril from the start. The first Mormons arrived in Britain's Cape Colony at Cape Town on April 19, 1853, but the mission was short-lived. The British and Dutch settlers were hostile to the missionaries' proselytizing and mobs sometimes attacked newly formed branches of the church. The mission closed in 1865 and many of the converts immigrated to Utah. When I asked the leader of my local church in Los Angeles about the prospect of danger, I was told that, yes, missionaries do die on their missions. But he assured me that such cases are rare and that, considering my age group as a whole, the safest place to be was on a mission.

I could have been called to any one of three hundred and thirty Mormon missions around the world, from Santiago to Seoul, San Antonio to St. Petersburg. The odds at that time were that I would work in a Spanish-speaking country. But I was called to South Africa. When I think about it now, it sounds like the makings of a musical – the great white missionary headed for Africa, from America, of all places. But at the time I didn't know quite what to think.

I worried about my mom. She had been stricken with breast cancer, which metastasized to her bones, making them as brittle as eggshells. Every day for her was a struggle with pain. And I would be nearly ten thousand miles from Los Angeles. Months later, already in South Africa, I learned of a situation in the 1980s similar to mine. A prospective young missionary in Oregon was very close to his mother. His local bishop had recommended to the Missionary Committee that he be assigned to a mission close to home so that his mother could phone weekly and visit him on occasion. He was sent to Johannesburg.

The leader of my church in Los Angeles, the stake president, had written to Thomas S. Monson, head of the Missionary Committee at that time and now president of the worldwide church, telling him that my mother would very likely die while I was on my mission and that I might want to return home for the funeral. Assigning me to South Africa obviously made that more difficult. I don't know if the church wanted to remove me from the painful circumstances of my mother's illness and likely death or take away the possibility of my returning for a funeral and then deciding not to go back to South Africa to resume my mission.

When we arrived in Cape Town, our passports were collected and kept by the mission president. The intention apparently was to keep me in South Africa, even if my mother died. But I decided on my own that I would stay, not because of the wishes of the church, but because my mother asked me to take up this mission and to complete it. I saw my staying as a tribute to her.

Despite my tentative experiments with drugs and sex, I was very naïve. At age nineteen, I was still an immature, spoiled-rotten California kid. My fellow missionaries and I were about to be thrust into the political cauldron of South Africa because all of us had supposedly been called by God to do His work at the Cape Town Mission. But I found out later that computer miscues and the cost of vehicles may have had more to do with the assignments than did God. After waiting six months for a Cape Town posting, eighteen of the twenty-four missionaries in our group attending the Missionary Training Center in Provo, Utah, were told before the start of training that their calls had been changed to Johannesburg, considered not nearly as cool as the vibrant port city at the southern tip of Africa. One unfortunate fellow, having already been relegated to Johannesburg, suffered a second disappointment when he was told during training that he was being re-diverted to a stateside mission in Detroit – unless he wanted to wait another six months for a Johannesburg assignment. He was understandably a bit down in the mouth.

"Jesus, I've already waited six months," he told me at the center, where the lot of us spent two and a half weeks being groomed "to embark in the service of God," as the center's motto declared. "No, I'll just go ahead and stay stateside and go to Detroit and get on with my life."

I learned later in South Africa that the people who ran the Cape Town Mission were able to pick and choose from the original group of twenty-four. "Because we definitely couldn't afford to buy ten new vehicles for twenty-four new missionaries," it was explained. So they chose six, based on their biographies, background checks and other stuff in their files.

I'm not sure how I made that list of six. I also didn't fully realize at the time that we were being sent into a war zone. The armored personnel carriers, townships in flame, human beings burned alive – all that news of mayhem that my mother and I had read in the paper the past summer. It didn't seem real; it hadn't been a part of my insulated life in Southern California. And here we were about to enter this violent, alien world.

South Africa, over the next two years, would be embroiled in what amounted to a civil war, leading to the historic one-man, one-vote multiracial elections in April 1994.

Shortly before I had left Los Angeles, the leader of my church in an LA suburb, a man with no experience with Africa whatsoever, laid his hands on my head in blessing and said: "Neal, you are being called to go and work with the black people in South Africa. You'll also work with some whites. They'll be hard-hearted, but they will be good people. But your mission and your success will be with the blacks."

I remember marveling at the revelation, thinking, this is what I want. This is exactly what I want and this is certainly meant to be. So when I arrived, I knew that I would go native. As the product of a U.S. education, I was taught nothing about South Africa, or even about Africa, for that matter. I didn't know a damned thing. But, as I promised my high school friend before I departed, my eyes were wide open. I was shivering with excitement about the adventures soon to unfold and felt mightily privileged to have landed, if only *just*, in the Republic of South Africa.

MOTHER CITY

CHAPTER TWO

The six of us who made the cut for the coolest postings flew on from Johannesburg to Cape Town where we were met by the mission leader, President Bingham, and his two missionary office clerks. As I walked off the tarmac with my new best friends, Elder Tague from Texas and Elder Stewart of Arizona, we were greeted by a towering bloke in a white shirt and black name tag that proclaimed him to be an "elder," just like us. He introduced himself and said he was our ride into the city. I'll call him Elder Young, because he was a direct descendant of one of the early prophets of the Mormon Church, such as the second president and founder of Salt Lake City, Brigham Young. But some members of his family probably would not want to see him associated with this story.

Young collected our bags and, although he couldn't have been much older than us, he said with the air of an old African hand, "Follow me, boys."

Tague, Stewart and I climbed into a mission Kombi,

a 1980s-vintage VW van. Young kicked the vehicle into high gear and maneuvered out of the airport and onto the wrong side of the road, as in Britain. The Kombi was a bit rough around the edges. Young slapped the steering column, as if to spur her forward, telling us she'd been one hell of a trooper, but would soon be retired – with honors.

He talked a mile a minute about how our first assignments were supposed to be confidential, but that he could divulge that four of us were staying in the Cape and two of us would travel to KwaZulu-Natal in the coming days. He said he was from Texas and had been on mission for nearly six months. He explained to us that the South Africa mission stretched from Natal on the east all the way around the Cape and up into Namibia in the west. He said it included about one hundred and fifty missionaries, not all of them young and doe-eyed like us.

"You're the first lot *not* to learn Afrikaans in the Missionary Training Center," he said. "On account of the black areas opening up with the lifting of the Group Areas Act. If you learn Xhosa, you'll do it here in South Africa – in the Cape or the Ciskei or the Transkei – in the black areas."

I asked about the possibility of going black. "Most missionaries," he said, "will serve three months in the black townships, but as you're new, if you're lucky, you'll see six."

A quarter of my mission, I thought. That would be brilliant.

As we drove along the motorway toward Cape Town, Young's face lit up in a big grin, and he pulled off onto a dirt path. It led to a shantytown, where he pulled up to a tin shack and parked. "Welcome to Africa," he said. "This is it – this is your new home."

The shack was falling in on itself, the paint on the rusting shingles once a bright green. I turned to Tague and Stewart. We figured it was a joke, but we played along, grabbing our bags as if to get out of the Kombi. We were "greenies." In the coming few weeks, any older missionary could mess us about, and all we could do was grin and take it – knowing it would one day be our turn to do the same to newcomers. This was an honor, we'd been warned in the Missionary Training Center. A tradition.

Before we could get out of the Kombi, Young stepped on the gas and pulled away from the shack. He laughed and told us that he and another missionary had recently been busted for playing an elaborate prank on some arriving greenies.

"This group wasn't like you," he said. "They were bookwormish and devout and they believed everything we told them. We left them at a house in the township with my companion and arranged for them to be robbed at gunpoint – without live ammo, of course – by some members of the church who looked like gangsters. They came into the house and grabbed the suitcases and fired blanks into my companion's stomach, which spurted fake blood. The newbies started screaming for the elders, for the missionaries to bless them, to save them, they later said, because that's all they could think of. And then, out of nowhere, we arrived. Some others and myself had doubled back after dropping them. We were hiding in the closets of the house and when they called out for help and we arrived instantaneously, they saw it as a sign from God. It was all so funny until President Bingham found out and said that we had destroyed their concept of mission and had scarred them for life, having ruined their first impressions of Africa."

"But, man," Young said as he pulled out of the shantytown and back onto the motorway, "if you could have only seen the looks on their faces. Priceless."

Young was larger than life for many reasons. I liked his unapologetic take on life. Others were deferential to him because of his family connection to Brigham Young. I would learn later he was somehow closer by blood to the founder of the church, Joseph Smith.

That first evening in the Cape, Young took us to the mission home in Pinelands, in Cape Town's southern suburbs, for a supper with the mission president and his wife, along with the assistants to the president, or APs, the mission's top missionaries. It was there that I learned – over a South African dinner of *bobotie*, a pie of spiced minced meat topped by frothy custard – that my first assignment would be in Lower Wynberg, a predominantly coloured area in Cape Town's southern suburbs. Stewart would report to the northern suburbs and Tague would fly on to Durban, a major port city on the Indian Ocean.

I asked the meaning of "coloured" because where I came from "coloured' was a derogatory term for black. It was explained to me that a "coloured" in South African parlance was a person of mixed race – halfway between a white and a black. And that while we, the whites, had to live in white-only areas, the laws had recently changed to the point where we could now cross over those boarders into the "coloured" and "black" areas, if only to preach.

* * *

I was pleased to be in Cape Town. I couldn't believe the beauty of the place. My jaw was on the floor all of the next day as Young took us on a whirlwind tour of the city, on to Cape Point where our Kombi was harassed by a troop of baboons, and then on to Clifton Beach No. 4, where partial nudity was allowed, and where I was accosted by a group of topless girls.

Young liked to bend the mission rules, especially when it came to girls, breasts and the ocean. One of our rules as missionaries – as set out in our little white handbook, known as our "White Bible," to be kept on our person at all times – was to never set foot in the ocean. It seems silly now, but I had been taught that the sea is the province of Satan.

> *Rule No. 46: Do not engage in water sports.*
> *Rule No. 55: Do not swim.*
> *Rule No. 76: Never associate inappropriately with anyone of the opposite sex.*

Young explained to us as we made our way onto the beach that these rules were largely technicalities. He let us in on a bit of mission lore – that Cape Town Mission "elders" (from

California, I'm proud to report) had introduced beach volleyball to South Africa, and that it was important to blend in with the locals when possible. "They'd taken it a bit far," Young said of those beach-loving Mormons, "spending the entirety of their mission on this very beach. So one morning out here for us shall readily be forgiven."

We nodded our appreciation and stripped down to our shorts (because we were too shy to go commando) and got ready for a pickup game of American football. Young shouted for us to go long, and he hurled the Styrofoam football ever closer to the sea. Some girls were frolicking in the breaking waves, their breasts bare and tanned and their smiles enticing. I'd plunge into the water to retrieve the ball and hurl it back to Young. He'd throw it again, farther out into the surf, each time closer to the girls.

"Do you speak Afrikaans?" one brunette girl called to me. She had detected our American accents as Young, Tague, Stewart and I had cavorted on the beach. I tossed the ball back to Young and approached her. As her giggly friends looked on, she beckoned me closer and put her arms around my neck.

"No, not a word," I confessed.

She told me to repeat after her, "*Goeie more, my bokkie.*"

Her language had a guttural tone, but, dammit, it sounded sexy. I looked to see if my fellow missionaries were watching and saw that Young was doubled over with laughter. But this temptress took hold of my head, and my privates, and captured my complete attention.

"*Goeie more, my bokkie,*" I repeated with a smile.

She'd been whispering into my ear, her lips brushing my neck and my ear, and now she leaned forward and kissed me on the mouth. After a lengthy embrace, we retreated with a mutual smile, our foreheads still touching.

"It means, 'Good morning, my little springbuck,'" she said.

The only response I could muster was, "Jesus Christ, I love this country."

* * *

A couple of days later, Forsythe P. Assante III was assigned as my
first missionary companion. By mission rules, he was to be my
shadow twenty-four hours a day. Assante came to Pinelands to pick
me up and take me to my mission area — Lower Wynberg — which
was "coloured" and more than ninety percent Muslim. I expected
that Assante would be black and hail from some obscure African
tribe. But he was white and from the U.S. West Coast, like me.

We traveled by bicycle along the railroad tracks, which
at that time divided the white and coloured areas. Assante was
from Washington state. He was blond like me and extraordinarily
carefree. He told me that, because this was my first day out,
I had to make the first contact. He led me to a door with a security
gate on the front of it and told me to knock hard.

A mosque was adjacent to the house. As I rehearsed my
speech in my head, Assante coached me a little on what to say. I
was to introduce myself, say where we came from, who we were
and so forth. As I started to knock on the door, a coughing rang
out, an exceptionally loud coughing and then a thundering sneeze,
amplified to an umpteenth degree. I realized that the noise was
coming from the next-door mosque, an exotic structure painted
moss green with white trim. It had a minaret with a loudspeaker
poking out the front. As the coughing and sneezing continued,
I realized this was meant to be a call to prayer, amplified by the
loudspeaker. But the imam had a head cold.

I nearly fell over laughing and thought this was the funniest
thing I had heard in my life, and what were the chances of having
to compete for attention at my first door with this: a sneezing,
wheezing imam — both of us engaged in the work of God? A
woman in a head wrap answered my knocks. At first she was
smiling, but her smile turned to a scowl as I tried without success
to suppress my laughing jag. Next door, the imam continued his
singsong of a prayer, punctuated with a hankering cough and a
sneeze. Forsythe P. Assante had to take over and explain to the

woman that I was new at this missionary stuff and was basically an idiot. But he told her we had been sent by God to speak to her. She slammed the door in our faces.

Assante gave me a *klap* across the face to bring me to my senses, and I shut the hell up. Further down the street, an older gentleman wearing a skullcap did let us in. But instead of us converting him, he just about converted us. He presented each of us with a decorative presentation copy of the Holy Quran and introduced his seven-year-old grandson, who, he said, could recite the entire book of scripture verbatim, from memory, "by the grace and gift of Allah."

We expressed amazement and asked how the boy had acquired such a talent. The grandfather explained that the Muslim community held an annual competition for kids. Each would step onto a stage and begin reciting the Quran, from line one, from the first page forward. One slip, and they'd be yanked off the stage.

"But not our Hakim," the grandfather said with a smile, patting the boy on the back. "The kid is going places. And if you're ever keen, he can teach you." The gap-toothed boy was all smiles, bashful but confident. I thought to myself: *Who the hell are we to go around preaching when there are people like Hakim who truly believe. People who know what's what for their own lives and aren't afraid to tell others about it.*

A bit later, after knocking on a few more doors, we ran into a coloured gang on the street who called themselves the JFK, aka the Junky Funky Kids. They were big on America and had loads of questions for us. They asked me if I'd ever run into a real live gang in LA and when I told them I was friends with the Mexican gang at my high school, the Whittier Vatos Locos, and the white gang, the Cactus Bunch, they seemed mightily impressed. I flashed the signs of these gangs for their amusement and they flashed their own signs in return and brandished their weapons so we could check them out. The lot weren't even packing guns – they had what appeared to be kitchen knives. It was odd because from what they told us about themselves, the Junky Funky Kids were meant to be tough, were meant to be ruthless killers, but they were giddy and friendly and incredibly cool with us.

Back across the tracks, we had some success at a Pick n Pay supermarket center, where a young white lady who owned a hair salon offered us cool drinks and ordered a tray of cookies.

Emma Coats had been seeing Mormon missionaries for a few weeks at that point, and from that very first meet and greet we hit it off famously. Emma was affable and liked to joke and had this great whooping laugh that reverberated into a snort. She lived with her family in the dozy seaside village of Kommetjie but worked in Plumstead, just across the street from our little flat. She was serious about the church but had doubts about going through with a baptism because her family were Seventh-day Adventists. They would disown her, she said, if she were baptized as a Mormon. Her sister, her parents and her grandmother would never speak to her again, she said. But I didn't believe it. I couldn't imagine anyone giving up on a natural-born talker like Emma, on the chance of a conversation with her.

Over the next couple of weeks our lessons concluded, and it came time for her to make up her mind. I met with Emma in private one Sunday after church, held her hands and told her of my mother. I gave her a photo of my mom and told her of Mom's struggles and said she truly believed. I asked Emma to set a date for her baptism. I pulled out my calendar and she chose at random a weekday evening a couple of weeks ahead, hoping that her family wouldn't find out. It would be my first baptism and I knew my mom would smile at the news.

* * *

Cape Town is called the Mother City. It's at the southern end of the African continent where Dutchman Jan van Riebeeck landed on April 8, 1652, to establish a settlement to grow vegetables and fruit to provision vessels bound for the Dutch East Indies. Over the past three and a half centuries it has grown into one of the world's most vibrant, cosmopolitan cities. And the Mother City would soon take on a maternal role in my personal life.

A month after my arrival in the Cape, the mission president and his wife paid a visit to our flat in Plumstead. It was late at night when they climbed the steps to the second floor and knocked on our door. Assante and I were going over plans for the next day. Another set of missionary companions who shared the flat with us answered the door. "I wonder what they want?" I whispered to Assante. Only something very important could bring both of the Binghams to our door at such an hour, and as the couple entered, Assante and I held this look, this awkward, awful, silent look, and we both knew.

The Binghams came in and sat down in our entryway/living room, both of them wearing solemn faces. We poured them some rooibos tea, a reddish brew made from a bush unique to South Africa. President Bingham, who had a head of gray, wavy hair, was retired, but he once owned one of the top accounting firms in Calgary, Alberta. His wife, Sister Bingham, was heavyset and the dominant member of the pair. She poked her husband, urging him to get to the point of their visit. But the president took his time. After a long, awkward pause as we sat sipping our tea, he said, "Elder Moore, we've come with bad news. Your mother has passed. And we'd like you to come back to the Mission Home to spend the night and be able to speak with your father on the telephone."

And so they drove me back in silence, back from Plumstead across the southern suburbs and into Pinelands where I sat down in a very empty, very lonely room and made the phone call through to my father. I was never any good speaking to my dad on the phone. I wished that I was back with Assante and that we could just go on doing what we had done the previous month. Attempting to speak to my dad, there was forever an indefinable stress that'd seep through the receiver, that'd reach through and take hold of me and squeeze my neck, without any words being spoken – that awkward feeling telling me how busy and businesslike and serious and anxious he was. But when I rang through he was sobbing on the other end of the line and I realized the call was as difficult for him to receive as it was for me to make. My father said that Mom had been upbeat to the end, that she had spent her last days at home in the hospital bed we'd set up downstairs, where I'd left her. He said that at the precise moment her spirit had departed, that everybody in the room knew that she had passed, there were two rose petals that fell from a bouquet of roses on her bedside table. And she was gone.

He told me the expected date of the funeral and asked what I wanted to do. I told him, "I won't make it back, father. My first baptism is actually going to be the same day. A young lady named Emma Coats."

Dad asked if I was sure. "Yes," I said. "I'm going to stay in my mom's honor, as she'd asked me to do."

* * *

What we did as missionaries, besides knocking on doors, which I eventually got better at, was something I liked a whole lot better. It was called nondenominational service. We'd take off our black name badges and just try to help out.

My first project was at a soup kitchen in Cape Town's central business district. We'd drive through to the old city center, put on aprons and serve soup to the indigent, to those who were having a hell of a struggle. They were white and black and coloured, all the colors of the Rainbow Nation to be. No race is immune from poverty and hardship. They would all smile and express their gratitude. A bowl of soup cost five cents, and a piece of bread a cent more, if I remember correctly. They'd line up, pitch their six cents into a bucket, lick their lips, and we'd deliver the goods.

During that time, I remember walking through the streets and back alleys of central Cape Town. I'd look up at all those old churches, all of that history, balconies with wrought-iron balustrades, gables galore, elaborate panels of pressed tin – colonial Africa as I had imagined it from reading books like Isak Dinesen's

Out of Africa, set in Kenya. But this was my new reality, a place that I could call home.

Looking up at Table Mountain on the odd occasion when the clouds would drape over its flat top like a tablecloth, I was overcome by the spectacular beauty of the city sparkling all about. I'd feel that I was enveloped, that I was completely enveloped by the love of the city center herself, along with the warmth of her people.

I'd asked my mom before I departed for Africa to send me a sign, if at all possible. To find a way to pull some strings (once she had passed), to let me know that she was OK and to help ensure that I wasn't going to be left all alone, that she'd be there right along with me, along for the ride. And so it was that my wish came true, although I'm still not sure to this day if I believe the way it worked itself out.

Emma Coats *was* baptized, as scheduled. She actually went through with it, after skipping our scheduled meetings just before the set date. I sat in the church on the night of her baptism, and took a moment away from the others after the deed had been done. I looked at my calendar and worked out the timing, taking into consideration the time difference between Cape Town and Los Angeles. And as it worked out – by chance, you might say – the exact moment when Emma was washed by the baptismal waters, my mom was laid to rest at Rose Hills Memorial Park in Whittier, California, the largest cemetery in the United States, in a plot next to my brother.

We had a little party for Emma at a friend's house to celebrate her big night. Between cool drinks and brownies and a whole lot of pudding, I took Emma aside in a hallway and asked what prompted her to be baptized.

"What happened, Emma?" I asked. "Why did you go through with this? I was so sure you wouldn't. What about your sister, what about your parents, your grandmother?"

And Emma was crying. She had this stunned look on her face and she was sobbing and it was hard to make out exactly what she was trying to say. But then she could speak and force her words out.

"Last night, I wasn't going to go through with it," she said haltingly, "and I knelt down to pray. But I couldn't because all I could think about was your mother, the picture that you gave me propped up by my bedside table. And that's when I heard a voice. It wasn't an inner voice, coming from within. And it wasn't a booming voice, like a voice outside my door. The voice was in the room, and the thing is, instead of being scared, I felt warm, and it felt good and it felt right."

I closed my eyes, not wanting to hear the rest. I knew quite well what the message was   the same thought my mother had voiced repeatedly during the summer before I left for Africa. But Emma was on a roll, and I couldn't have stopped her if I'd tried.

"The voice was of a woman," Emma said. "And she was repeating, over and over and over again, 'I am so proud of my son.'"

SIYABONGA

CHAPTER THREE

Walking about the City of Cape Town, in a city that was still divided by race, between the first, second, and third classes – between the whites, the coloureds, and the blacks – my mind shifted back to my own experience in my own home country, in my own home city, understanding for the first time that we as Americans were likewise a culture divided by race and divided by boundaries, divided by the haves and the hopefuls and the have-nots. We didn't call it *Apartheid* in Los Angeles; we didn't call it anything – we just pointed the finger in the general direction of anywhere but ourselves when the word "racist" came into play.

My only previous experience with anybody who was black in Los Angeles, besides once attending private school with a relative of Nat King Cole, was with our maid – my mother's nursemaid – by the name of Rayshine.

Rayshine was African-American and I loved her with all my heart. Together, a couple of years previous, we had gone to select a Christmas tree and I had chosen the largest tree on the Christmas tree lot, one that was sprinkled over in fake white snow, that had been frosted, so to speak. And Rayshine, who was small but wiry, helped me hoist it up onto my car and we tied it down and we were able to bring it back to the house where it fit just perfect because my boyhood home in LA was of a good size. The thing is that without my brother and with the possibility of it being the final Christmas with my mom, and all, I was trying to fill a space that was impossible to fill, when I think about it properly, now. But this had been a good go, a good substitute, for the time being. And it looked just fine.

Now when I was a child at Christmastime we were allowed to open one present on the night before Christmas and then you had to wait until Christmas morning for the rest. And leading up to Christmas that year I remember, on one of her off days, Rayshine invited me to visit her house and so I went with her and I was really excited to meet her family. I must have been about seventeen years old and we drove into the projects of South-Central Los Angeles and when I realized what kind of a neighborhood we had pulled ourselves up to, I asked her whether it was safe to get out of the car and she said, "Yeah, child, absolutely, you're okay – you're with me – we're going to see my family."

She had come prepared with a basket full of fruit and it was wrapped up nicely and this was her Christmas present to her family. And as we traversed the steps up of what's referred to as a *project*, or government formed apartment block, in Los Angeles – this particular area predominately African-American – we came into the apartment in question, into her family's home, and before the basket could make its way down, could descend onto the top of that living room table, children from out of nowhere came running and rustling and whistling over and their hands were up and into the basket. Before it hit the table all of the fruit was gone, everything inside the basket was gone, and I stood there in abject horror, half of my mind thinking, *Dammit, they didn't wait for Christmas*, and the other half realizing, *Holy hell, these people are hungry,* and this is how the poor live. And this was something that I had had no experience with, whatsoever.

* * *

Walking around Cape Town was an eye-opener on multiple levels. I was living in a white area just across the railroad tracks from a coloured area. The schools for white children in the southern suburbs of Cape Town resembled the best prep schools on America's East Coast. Like the school in the 1989 movie *Dead Poets Society,* they had multiple sports fields and old, solid buildings with ivy creeping up the walls.

In the coloured area, where I worked, there wasn't a single bit of greenery. Everything was cemented over. I walked up and down every street in Lower Wynberg, knocked on most of the doors and got to meet a lot of people. There was one school, right in the center. It had a tall fence, topped with barbed wire, all around it. The playground was devoid of grass, all cement.

And then there were the black areas, the townships filled with government housing on the outskirts of Cape Town. I was once taken into the black township of Gugulethu by a white member of the church who was a policeman. His job was driving a police Casspir, one of those gargantuan, beast-like machines used to suppress unrest in the townships. The yellow anti-riot vehicle with a wide blue stripe down its sides had over-sized tires, armor plating and slits for automatic weapons to point their way out, down and onto the crowds of those times. My ride-along, I was told, violated police and mission rules, so I was not to mention it to anybody – especially to mission leaders – because it was bound to get back to the police.

The driver for the ride-along, Feliks Blaf-nou, as his friends called him, a great big monster of a bloke, was in charge of the biggest vehicle in the police fleet, the tow-truck Casspir. It looked like a regular Casspir from the front, but it was extended with a gigantic crane of a wrecking ball of a hitch on the back. He told us his job was "separating black-on-black violence," like he was doing the citizenry of the township a favor, but according to the reception we received that day in Gugulethu, I'd have to politely disagree. Occasionally a Casspir would catch on fire or be immobilized while trying to separate native unrest, Feliks explained, and this gent would accelerate his beast of burden into the fray and tow-up the crippled, disabled Casspir in question, saving the day and towing it out of the danger zone.

Rule No. 154: Be conscious of safety at all times.
Rule No. 155: Drive defensively.
Rule No. 156: Pray for the Lord's protection while driving.

On that day in late 1991, when we drove into the danger zone of Gugulethu, some residents skipped out of the way, some ignored us, and some glared at the vehicle and saluted with their middle fingers. Others hurled stones and shouted, "Fuck off!" and "Fuck you!" We were insulated by steel and glass and their shouts were muffled, but it was easy enough to figure out what they were saying. There was anger and fear in the eyes of the teenagers that I saw from up high in our rolling fortress in the sky. It was patently clear that we were not welcome.

On our drive through Gugulethu, we passed a low, flat-roofed building with broken windows. It was a school, but no children were around. Schools had become particular targets of violence in black areas of South Africa because lessons were on occasion taught in Afrikaans, the language of the oppressors. Also, school facilities were extremely primitive. Classrooms had no electricity, so kerosene lanterns were used to provide light. They offered no encouragement, no future, no hope.

Aboard the Casspir, the driver showed me where bullets had hit the windscreen, pinpointing where automatic weapons had hit the glass too close to where I was sitting. "If AK-47 fire hits this bulletproof glass one time, you're fine," he said. "If it hits it for a second time in the exact same spot, you're fucked, you're totally fucked and the window is going to explode."

Feliks told me that of course it had happened, that his windows had been shattered, but that you get on with it and attempt to live another day. He didn't say as much, but I could see in his eyes as we arrived back at our flat in Plumstead, that he was living in fear, like other whites in this beleaguered, divided country.

* * *

At night in our flat, we'd sometimes have visits from other members of the church. We seemed to attract cops and soldiers. Geldenhuis, an ex-soldier in his early to mid-thirties, would tell stories late into the night of his experiences in the Angolan Bush War. That nasty conflict along the border between the South African-ruled territory of South-West Africa and Angola ended in 1989 and led to independence in 1990 for South-West Africa, renamed Namibia. The bush war pitted the South African Defence Forces against guerrillas of the South-West Africa People's Organisation (SWAPO) who used Angola as a sanctuary. Geldenhuis was clearly affected by the war. He'd sometimes go into a trance-like state when he'd speak, sounding the words out at times when it was too difficult or too painful to conjure up the memories, settling down into a mumble of a monotone once he'd at long last get going, the lot of us missionaries in the flat gathered around, hands up on our heads or folded across our legs in contemplation, our imaginations running rampant, attempting to share his pain. We sat in the flat enthralled by stories that painted the war as a hell on earth. He told of killing guerrillas and of comrades being killed. He related stories about hush-hush operations, of whole villages being eliminated by fragmentation bombs or artillery on the basis of coordinates that he had called in as a special forces "recce," or recon commando. He now had to live with these memories. Maybe one way he dealt with his psychological turmoil, which would now be called PTSD, or post-traumatic stress disorder, was to tell his tales to strangers from a foreign land. Maybe he saw us – missionaries – as confessors and our flat as a confessional.

I once asked Geldenhuis what he thought about the situation at home, in South Africa – if he thought the country was on the verge of a race war. He told me what I'd heard from many other whites in the Cape – that they'd be fine as long as the Zulus didn't rise up. During colonial times, both the Zulus and the whites had won major battles – the Zulus at Isandlwana and the whites at Rorke's Drift. There seemed to be a mutual respect between the whites and the Zulus, a people known for their prowess in war. "We've got the weapons, we've got the training, and we've got the armaments," Geldenhuis said. "But goddammit, they've got the spears and the pangas and the will. Just as long as we don't meet the Zulus, we'll be OK."

* * *

I knew that my mission wouldn't keep me with the Cape coloureds or among the whites. I knew that eventually I would "go black," as we called it. It was a move that I hoped for. To push things along, I asked for "splits" – an "exchange" with a missionary other than my daily companion – with one of the assistants to the president. I knew that when they weren't helping President Bingham around the mission, they worked in Gugulethu, known affectionately as "Gugs."

I had been going through a tough time after the death of my mom, and one of the assistants to the president had been very kind. His name was Hall, a white South African who had already served twenty-three months of his mission and was on his way out. "*Ja*, absolutely," he said to my request to work with him. So one morning he drove to my flat to pick me up. We shook hands and he said, "Elder Moore, we're going to have a prayer together. We're going to study together, and then I'm going to take you for the day into my area, Gugulethu. Then I want you to tell me how I can improve, how I can be a better missionary."

I knew he was just being kind, but I was dumbfounded by his generosity, by taking the time out of his busy schedule to accompany me, a greenie, into his area. He knelt in prayer, closed his eyes and asked for guidance and protection, that we would be led to people who would want to listen to us.

As we drove into Gugulethu, he said, "Neal, first of all, there are a few things we absolutely have to do – a rite of passage on your first day in the township."

I nodded innocently, not about to tell him that I'd been down this very road not long ago, in a Casspir.

"We have to introduce you to smiley, we have to get you a smiley, first and foremost," he said, "and we have to get you a name."

Now this I had not done, and I realized this was something grander than the Casspir, something that could never transpire between armor plating and automatic weapons and the possibility of bulletproof windows.

We drove to an intersection of two dirt paths, where some rotund Xhosa women, in colorful garb and head wraps, were huddled around a big black cauldron, stirring the bubbling contents. We parked and approached the ladies, and Hall ordered a smiley. They smiled.

I asked what a smiley was, and one of the ladies said it was a sheep's head, hoisting one out of the boiling vat. A favorite food among the Xhosa and Zulu people, smileys are prepared by stripping a whole sheep's head of as much hair as possible, washing it and boiling it in a large pot. The head is then roasted over hot coals. As the head turns a golden brown, the intense heat shrinks the lips into what looks like a grisly smile. Hence the name smiley.

The ladies wrapped a smiley in newspaper and we drove to the house of a church member in the township to share our bounty with his family. As we sat round the large dining room table, I was urged to take an eyeball, which along with the cheek meat is a choice morsel of a smiley. I popped it into my mouth and the kids asked how it tasted. "Like chalk," I said. And of course we all smiled.

Hall ate the other eyeball and kissed his fingers as a compliment to the chef. "The best meat, Elder Moore," he explained to me, "is just around the eye socket, as that meat had been in motion and is more tender, along with the meat just behind the ears." From there, we drove to another house in the township, the tidy home of a very large woman whose size and demeanor demanded attention. And in her community, it was apparent, she was a person who commanded respect, even reverence.

"This is Neal Moore," explained Elder Hall. "He is from America, and he needs to have a name."

With considerable pomp, the woman, draped in an elaborate, well balanced kikoy cloth getup from head to toe, brought out a large, intricately carved chair and set it before me in her main room, whose walls were painted bright blue and red and gave off an odor of mustiness and kerosene. I thought that I was supposed it sit in the chair, but as I tried to take a seat, the woman's neighbors who had gathered in the room motioned for me to stand in front of the chair as she adjusted it, just so. "What is his name? Moore?" the woman asked as I stood, waiting for some sort of ceremony to begin. Other neighbors streamed into the room, having heard that something worth watching was about to happen. I looked toward Elder Hall, who stood off to the side, his arms folded with a big grin on his face.

"*HLALA PHANTSI! HLALA PANTSI!* SIT DOWN!" the woman shouted. As I sat, she stood behind me. I turned around, curious as to what would happen next. The woman's eyes were closed tightly, her head was rolling from side to side and she was shifting back and forth on her feet as she began the naming ceremony. "YOU ... ARE ... SIYABONGA!" she yelled, sounding out the syllables in a rolling cadence that sounded like poetry.

It was a bedazzling event. In the hushed room after the woman made her pronouncement, the heads of the neighbors nodded in acceptance, as if to say, "Yes, this is correct. This young man is clearly a Siyabonga." Then they began to whoop and holler and applaud.

Still seated, tears welled in my eyes. My head buzzed from the intensity of the ceremony and because of the warmth of acceptance emanating from this formidable woman and others in the room. I was happy and grateful. When I was told that I could stand, the woman wrapped her arms around me like a huge mother bear, and I hugged her all the harder right back.

"What does *Siyabonga* mean?" I asked. She stepped back, still holding my shoulders, and proclaimed, "We are thankful."

I swallowed hard and realized I had a lot to live up to with such a name, in such a place in the world. I nodded to indicate that I would give it my best, that I would unflinchingly sally forth, that I would walk away from my past experience of one culture and one religion and open myself up to all of the experiences and people I would encounter in this strange, new environment. And I tried to get out the words that *I* was thankful to be here and thankful for her. But she wasn't finished.

"We are thankful for you, that you are here," the woman said, still shifting back and forth on the balls of her feet and speaking as if she were making a proclamation. "We are thankful for you coming to South Africa. We are thankful for you coming into the township. We are thankful for you opening yourself up and into our hearts."

HOMELAND
IN FLUX

GRAND-PA
HEADACHE POWDERS

CHAPTER FOUR

Before my family moved inland from Seal Beach, along the Southern California coast, my mother had a dream – a vision of sorts. She woke up one morning, around the time she came down with cancer, and said she had dreamed that we were going to live next to a cemetery.

We had moved house for various reasons about every two years from the time I'd been born – all over the San Fernando Valley, West Los Angeles and Orange County. So this was nothing new. We'd lived behind the home of comedian Richard Pryor at the time he'd set himself alight. We'd lived amongst the hustle and bustle of the cityscape of Westwood Village near the UCLA campus. And we'd lived amongst the surfers at Seal Beach. But a graveyard? Albeit macabre, that was novel. As a kid, I viewed such a move as a new adventure. But I should have known better. I should have seen the dream as the omen it most certainly was.

Nearly a year after we moved to Whittier, next to the cemetery, my brother, Tom, was involved in a serious accident. He was sixteen then, and I was thirteen. Tom had lost control of his 1985 Mustang GT on some dry leaves on a winding road in the foothills above LA. Four other kids were in the car, including his girlfriend, Debbie Lin. They all survived. But Tom suffered traumatic whiplash, along with injuries to his head and body. He was in a coma for ten days after the accident, until there was no hope and he was taken off life support. When I first saw him in ICU, I wasn't prepared for the gravity of his condition. I knew he had been in a wreck, but I imagined he'd be lying in the hospital bed with his leg propped up in a cast and waiting to greet me with a lame joke. I planned to poke fun at him for getting himself into such a mess. But within moments of approaching his battered, comatose form, my legs buckled and I fell to the floor. I began to kick and scream, the reality of it, the finality of his situation crashing down all round me, the sudden realization that he most sincerely wasn't OK. The nurses had to restrain me in a padded room until I could control my emotions.

Our latest home, fortunately, was not far from his gravesite at Rose Hills. Often after I had finished my classes in junior high school, when I was thirteen and fourteen, I'd hop on my bicycle and ride to a roadside Mexican flower stand where I had a standing order for a single white rose. I would then pedal, with rose in hand, to Rose Hills Memorial Park to our family's bit of earth, high up on the hill in Deseret Lawn, set aside for people of the Mormon faith. There, I would sit on a patch of grass next to the grave of my brother and gaze out at the San Gabriel Mountains and, on smog-free days, the skyline of downtown Los Angeles. The place where I sat was intended to be my gravesite one day, and sometimes I'd wish that I were already there, dead and buried and six feet under.

* * *

I had idolized Tom. He was handsome, popular with his peers and drove that flashy Mustang, white with red interior. I had tried to follow him from the time I could walk. During the last of his sixteen years, he'd sometimes take me along on outings with his friends. Occasionally, just the two of us would drive through the neighborhoods where we used to live, or along the Pacific Coast Highway, where I'd silently will him to slow down and not drive so very fast.

Tom was a hell-raiser. During his short life he seemed to model himself on an iconic Southern California rebel of an earlier generation, James Dean. And, in turn, he was a formative influence on my own life. Looking back, not all of it was good. After his death, I learned that he had crammed a lot of living into his sixteen years. He smoked, drank, slept with a variety of high school classmates and even adult women. And, much to the chagrin of our mother, he didn't try to hide his non-Mormon-like behavior. In fact, he had made an appointment to have his name removed from the membership rolls of the Church of Jesus Christ of Latter-day Saints. His auto accident was on a Friday night. The appointment was for the following Sunday. Near the end of Tom's ten days on life support, the bishop of our church came to the hospital to pray over him. "There is something worse than physical death," the bishop told our family, "which Tom wasn't able to go through with on account of the timing of his accident." The bishop said that Tom was still in good standing with the church. So he died a Mormon, but I knew better. My brother lived and died on his own terms. He had been his own person, and I respected him for it.

About five hundred mourners, many of them high school classmates, attended Tom's funeral service at Rose Hills. I gave the eulogy and somehow finished it without breaking down. Soon afterward, I began to drink coffee, a taboo for Mormons, and stronger drinks, like Jack Daniels, Tom's favorite. Tom's best friend, Andy Lin, Debbie's brother, took me under his wing and would let me sleep at his house, higher up on the hill from our home. He told me I should sleep on my side if I was drunk so that I wouldn't choke on my vomit if I threw up in my sleep. During this time, I also began experimenting sexually with girls. I guess I saw it as homage to Tom, as if he were looking on from heaven — or wherever — and approving.

But it was more than his rebelliousness that made me idolize Tom. Not long before he died, my brother was arrested by the Whittier police, accused of a hit-and-run accident. Whittier High School allowed students to leave the campus for lunch, as did Tom one day with his Mustang full of friends. Racing to get back before the start of afternoon classes, the car careered on two wheels to the front of the school and screeched to a stop. Passengers piled out and ran for class. The Mustang, well known on campus, hit and dented the bumper of an unoccupied vehicle as it made its departure in search of a parking spot near the school. The whole thing was witnessed by a plainclothes cop named Phil. We called him a narc because his main mission, mostly fruitless, was to ferret out drugs. That afternoon Tom was led out of class in handcuffs. My dad picked me up at my junior high and we drove to the police station to meet the family lawyer. Tom was locked in a cell with a scary-looking guy who police said had raped and killed an old woman. All Tom had to do to be freed, I was told, was to give a statement to the police. But he wouldn't say anything. Late that night, Jimmy Wu, a Taiwanese American friend who lived up the hill from us near the Lins, appeared at the police station with his father. It was then that we got the real story. Jimmy had been driving the Mustang when it hit the parked vehicle. But Tom hadn't said a word. He wouldn't rat on his friend and was prepared to take the fall if Jimmy hadn't found the courage to tell his dad. I admired Tom for that. He was loyal to his friend, and, in my eyes, not afraid of anything.

* * *

One afternoon at Rose Hills, as I sat sobbing at Tom's grave and thinking about our times together, a stunningly beautiful woman walked toward me after a funeral service she had attended amid a row of headstones not far from our plot. She had blonde hair and an air of sophistication in her step. I was embarrassed for her to see me in such a state, until I noticed her own tear-smudged face. She had seen that I was crying, sitting on the grass, my arms cradling my legs. She clutched a rose that had been intended for the descending casket at the graveside service she had just attended. She was apparently confronting her own grief as she stopped to consider me. She smiled through her tears and, without a word, she handed her rose to me. Her poignant gesture told me that she understood, that my grief was now shared.

By the time I was fifteen, I had made up my mind how I would do it. I would off myself with drugs. I wasn't going to sample or dabble or start out with a gateway drug. I was going to graduate early on, and dive right into cocaine – into an extraordinarily large amount of cocaine. It wasn't meant to be anything spectacular or sensational or something to brag to my school friends about, to tell a single living soul. It was simply meant to be the end.

When that fateful day arrived, I made my purchase at school, rode my bike to Deseret Lawn at Rose Hills, took one last look at the mountains and the LA skyline and then rode home. I went into my brother's bedroom, which was exactly as he'd left it, and looked at the framed photos of us on the wall, in happier times. That gave me courage. And then to the bathroom, which we had shared, between our respective rooms, where I closed and locked the door. I had always felt small and alone in this large house. And I didn't want to be alone anymore. I dumped the white, powdery substance onto the sink counter and used a razor blade to line up what I thought to be a lethal dose, followed by a second line, just to make sure. I rolled a crisp bill, as I'd seen done in the movies, brought it to my nose, and snorted the entire lot – first one line and then the other. I fell back onto the tile floor, my gums numb and tingly, my body twitching with delight, my young mind trying to focus on the ceiling above. But I soon realized that I was still alive. I had failed in my mission.

OK, you'll have to live, I told myself. *But it's not going to be pretty.*

I tried to put a stop to this death wish, and my reckless and sloppy efforts to fulfill it. But I couldn't.

Maybe it was guilt – that I was alive and my brother was dead, that he would have led a better life than me. Nearly every day, whether morning, afternoon or evening, the same drama would present itself forward. My mind would settle into a place where I was confident and fearless and, most important, where I didn't give a fuck about anything, about what happened to me. Friends would try to throw away or flush my stash, and I'd laugh, and say, "There's more where that came from. You can't stop me!"

But privately I'd beg my dealer, the kid who sat next to me in social studies, to stop selling to me. He'd nod in agreement, and say, "Yeah, you're fucked, Neal. You've got yourself a real problem." I'd dab my bleeding nose with a handkerchief, and he'd produce more. He had the product and I had the money. I'd sometimes snort a line in the middle of a class of forty students, on my wooden folding desk. I thought it was funny because the teacher was oblivious, just like my parents. Once the kid sold me what I learned later was a bad batch. I saw double, and my clothes were soaked in sweat. I stumbled out of the classroom with both hands out in front of me, the world spinning to one side and then to the other, and finally upside down.

My parents were hardly aware of my inner turmoil. I think they meant well, but were distant, both preoccupied with their careers. My father owned a high-dollar accountancy firm. He and his wealthy clients collaborated on real estate developments all over California, which required him to be away a lot. Tax-preparation season was even worse. At that time of year, he lived in an apartment in the building that housed his firm in Long Beach. He never spent much time with me as a child. During baseball season, when I'd have to go to practice after school, one of his secretaries usually drove me to the field.

My mother was also frequently away from the home. She taught special-needs children in various schools, and went to night classes to earn multiple degrees in her field. One of her master's degrees, from Cal State Los Angeles, focused on the use of computers in teaching special-needs kids. My mom's earlier career, before Tom and I were born, was as a professional dancer. Her parents had come to the United States from Blantyre, Scotland, the home of the famous Scottish missionary Dr. David Livingstone. She was born in Los Angeles, where the family had settled. South-Central LA, where they lived, was the home of many Scottish immigrants before African Americans began moving into the area in the 1940s. My mother became involved in Scottish dancing, performed at local Gaelic festivals, appeared on Betty White's radio show and on local TV, and also taught dance. As a girl, she spent two summers in Blantyre with her grandmother. That's how she learned the Scottish lullabies she crooned to me as a child.

* * *

In South Africa, after my mother's death, I became afraid of myself, of the demons that still haunted me, of how I would cope with her absence in my life, of how I would fill the void that was growing bigger every day.

This zeal for mission work could only last so long, I thought to myself. It was great when I was out in the township, feeling like I was doing good work in fulfillment of my mother's wish. But then things would change. Someone might say or do something to set me off. It might be something like an elderly white lady shaking her cane at me and complaining that we mustn't ride our bicycles on the sidewalk, going on to yell, "I know who you are. You believe in the Book of the Normans. You give out bibles or something stupid like that." Then the bright noonday sun would turn as dark and foreboding as the old lady's scowl.

There was a bottle store around the corner from our flat in Plumstead. I longed for a drink more than anything, but I couldn't bring myself to seek any solace there, under the noses of the other missionaries – until, that is, they looked the other way.

But slugs from a 350ml bottle of vodka, chased by a breath mint, weren't good enough. They didn't ease the pain. And I knew if I kept sneaking out of the flat at night to visit the bottle store and squirreling away my stash of spirits, I'd eventually get caught. My fellow missionaries may have been naïve, but they weren't stupid. And they were concerned.

I wish there were a way to sugarcoat this episode in my life, but there wasn't. Until I stumbled upon the idea of Grand-Pa Headache Powders, a popular over-the-counter painkiller. The stuff was advertised on local TV. It came in paper packets and was white and coarse and powdery. I knew it was, essentially, only aspirin, but I liked to think of it as high-grade coke.

And so with Assante in tow, I went to a nearby pharmacy, claiming to have one hell of a headache. I bought all of the shop's large packets of Grand-Pa Headache Powders. The pharmacist remarked, to take care, that the stuff could be addictive, and I thought, well, that's fine with me. Back at the flat, I went into the bathroom and locked the door, as I had done at my home in LA. I arranged long lines of the powder on the countertop. It looked just like cocaine, and I ingested it through my nose, re-enacting the suicidal impulses of my earlier years.

Now, it all seems childish and a bit bizarre. Was it cowardice? Was I engaging in this pathetic pantomime of suicide out of a desire to be with my brother and mother, but not really wanting to die?

How ridiculous am I? I asked my reflection in the bathroom mirror, as I'd neatly arrange another line of Grand-Pa Headache Powders on the sink counter.

I played this silly game for some time, until I got bored with it. The headache powder wasn't cocaine, of course, and it was doing nothing to ease my pain. I needed something *real*.

* * *

One night after my flatmates had drifted off, breathing deeply in the solitude of their sleep, I slid out of bed and reached for my backpack. I removed my nametag and tie, stuffed pillows and other odds and ends under my blanket to make it appear I was tucked snugly in bed and tiptoed out the back door, which we never locked.

It was late as I walked up the dark street in search of somebody to smoke with. I was feeling down and dirty and basically in need of a screw as I hailed a passing taxi and asked the driver, "Where can I go for a lady of the night? I have money."

He tipped his cap and we headed toward Sea Point, once a whites-only suburb but now becoming a place to find drugs and prostitutes. We raced along the M5 motorway, rounded a sharp bend on Signal Hill and up into Sea Point. The taxi stopped in a parking lot next to a building with a flashing neon sign. I paid the driver, gave him some extra cash to wait for me and nodded my way past the bouncer at the front doors.

"A house of ill repute," I uttered to myself as I pushed through the doors. Just inside, a woman curtsied and introduced herself as having come from Sweden.

I'd had a similar experience in my seventeenth year with a cousin in England, and thought this establishment might be similar – a place to see a lap dance and some cavorting around a pole. But the woman took me by the hand and led me on a tour of three rooms.

Rule No. 75: Never be alone with anyone of the opposite sex.
Rule No. 77: Do not flirt.
Rule No. 78: Do not date.

"This is the S&M room," the woman explained, showing me a bed equipped with handcuffs and a wall hung with thick leather belts. "And this is the Greek-style room," she said, prompting me to ask, "What the fuck is that?" But she only smiled, and carried on with the tour. "And this is the room where you can have a private audience with myself."

"I'll go for the private audience," I said, not quite able to get the words out fast enough.

But first, the Swede was off to perform a one-woman show for several customers. So I waited at the bar and asked the barman how things worked at this place.

"What do you want? A half-hour or an hour with the lady?" asked the barman, who sported multiple tattoos and a friendly smile. He was a guy who had seen it all, including naïve kids out to prove their manhood.

"I'll invest in an hour," I said.

"And what about for these ladies at the bar, for their drinks while you wait?"

The bar was full of bona fide prostitutes, who flirted and smiled and, all of a sudden, looked awfully thirsty. I asked for whiskeys all around and the barman said, "Ta," and began to pour.

A group of English gents with loosened ties and cheap business suits, who had been watching the Swede perform upstairs, filed past me on the way out. One of them slapped me on the shoulder and proclaimed, "If I can tell you one thing, young man, if I can impart to you just a little bit of wisdom and good sense that woman's a lady in *all* respects. She's a pro and definitely hot and knows exactly what she's doing."

I patted the man on the back as he passed. "Not to worry," I smiled. And he was off, out the front doors with his mates, whistling as they went.

They've got to be husbands, they've got to be fathers, I thought to myself. *But how much more of a hypocrite am I?*

The Swede took me to the third room and closed the door behind us, and I no longer cared. There was a bed and an array of candles and up on the bureau, a pile of fine-grade beautiful green buds. I pointed to the *dagga* and she raised her index finger as if to say, "Wait," and reached for a pipe.

She was wearing hardly anything to begin with, but she took off her panties and bra and started to undress me. Her nipples hardened as I reached out to embrace her, but she wagged her finger and whispered, "No."

This woman had a gift when it came to undressing a customer, nice and slow and sexy as hell. One button at a time until my shirt was off, my trousers halfway down. She never lost eye contact, her face wearing a forced smile. And I recognized that smile; I'd seen it before. In the heat of the room, the Swede's makeup had run, and what I saw was a smile of pain.

My mind raced back to that day on Deseret Lawn at Rose Hills Memorial Park, to that blonde, older woman who approached me at my brother's grave. I thought of her sad smile, and how it had haunted me. I thought of my brother smiling a genuine, encouraging smile, and my mother, frowning in disapproval – and I couldn't do it.

The Swede reached for my drawers, but I brought my hands down to stop her.

"I just want to smoke," I said, and she nodded, reaching up to brush away a tear running down my cheek.

I pushed down my pants, and my underwear garments, and stepped out of them, the two of us back on the bed, against a plethora of cushions, as if to consider. The Swede lit the pipe as we sat back together and took long drags, passing the pipe back and forth.

She laid her head on my bare shoulder for what seemed like an eternity. I smoked and I smoked as she laid there nice and content, for a good long while. And as I smoked I began to mellow out, to feel an easing of the pain that had boxed me in. And I realized that, indeed, I would in fact live another day.

I couldn't stand it any longer, and I reached for her breasts. She reached for me and expertly rolled a condom onto my *piel*. I lunged on top of her, and into her, but she turned and rolled me onto my back, pinning my hands behind my head as she eased herself down and onto me, nice and slow and proper.

I closed my eyes as half of my brain rejoiced, thinking, "So *this* is what Joseph Smith was talking about! Epiphany! This is that place – this is the *real* religion!" While the other half of my mind froze, as I thought, "Jesus, this is an X-rated movie unfolding before my very eyes — a cock and a cunt pounding harder and faster — and I'm quite sure I'm not allowed to watch!"

The woman collapsed on top of me, excused herself, and my skin felt coarse. I felt as if I had lost something. It wasn't my virginity; that was already gone. But I wasn't as innocent as I'd been when I'd waltzed into this place a little over an hour before.

I didn't quite look at the world the same as I buttoned up my clothes, my heart suddenly heavy and weighted down like a stone. As I descended the stairs and made my way out and onto the street, the sky shone down silver in the first light of a new day.

A PINE BOX

CHAPTER FIVE

Mission transfers, they called them: Routine paper shuffling for the mission leaders, a shifting of the stars and the planets for the missionaries. It happened at the start of every month. In an ideal world, a missionary was supposed to work for six months in a specified area, with a total of two companions, each serving for three months. But it hardly ever worked out that way.

What I hadn't taken into consideration was *whom* I would be walking with, not too far down the road. That Assante wouldn't be there forever to show me the ropes, to encourage me, to correct me. I had no idea how lucky I'd been to know him, to have been assigned to the guy, as his replacement would be a totally different story, a different animal, all together.

Come the end of the month, a handful of missionaries from the Cape Town Mission would be outbound upon the conclusion of their twenty-four-month missions. A matching number of newbies would be inbound, from North America and/or South

Africa, ready and willing to take their places. While the rest of us who still had time remaining on mission would be wide open for the potential of a transfer, mission-wide.

The assistants to the president would sit down with President Bingham around mid-month before a "transfer board" in the mission headquarters. It was a large wooden board, normally locked away and out of sight. It bore photographs of every missionary, the lot of us smiling down from the board, pleading to be sent to a new area, or to remain. For those hoping for a transfer, Namibia was a favorite destination. Once a German colony, later ruled by South Africa and now an independent country, Namibia was favored for its remoteness from the centers of mission authority. But the black townships were prized above all because they offered so few slots for missionaries and for the opportunity to learn the Xhosa language.

So at transfer time, we missionaries would wait anxiously for decisions on our fate. Were we going to stay in our present assigned area or push off to the next *endroit exotique*? Late in the wee hours of the morning, the news would arrive via a series of telephone calls, trickling their way down the mission chain of command. The APs, or assistants to the president, would telephone the zone leaders, ZLs, who in turn would phone the district leaders, DLs. The district leaders, responsible for the smallest of the units, such as a city suburb, would then sit down with their underlings to impart the news from on high.

That's how I learned that Forsythe P. Assante was being transferred to Cape Town's northern suburbs, out Paarl-way in the Cape's wine-growing region, and that a character named Clapp was on his way in. I would have loved to stay with Assante. And was a little saddened and dismayed that he appeared happy to pack up his bags and push off to his new assignment. Suddenly filled with regret, I thought back to how I might have been a better companion, a better missionary. We shook hands, he said he'd look out for me at the Cape Mission meetings held every couple of months, and then he was gone.

The first thing I noticed when Clapp showed up was that he wore black leather gloves, matching his tousled black hair. At first I thought they were bicycle gloves, but then I realized he wore them to hide the fact that he was missing two and a half fingers on his right hand.

Clapp liked to shake hands, and when he did, his grip was twice as hard as necessary. He'd size you up with his head askew, watching for a reaction to the odd sensation of shaking a nub, with pincers.

He seemed nice enough, at first. What I didn't know about Clapp was that he was supposed to be taking medication to curb his propensity for violence. That, and I wouldn't find out until months later that, during this particular stint of his mission, he'd made the unilateral decision not to do so.

So Assante was out and Clapp was in. With little in the way of introductions, he swept into the flat, plopped himself onto Assante's old bed, pulled the sheets up over his head and settled in for a nap.

"It's a transfer day," he said. "We'll work tomorrow."

Bright and early the next morning, I brewed us some tea, paced the floor and ostentatiously tapped my watch, as if to ascertain the correct time, all the while holding a determined look on my face, like when the *hell* are we headed out, because this is what I loved to do. What I needed. I needed to be out of doors, because I was attempting to justify to myself a reason to stay on my mission. And it was not to be bottled up inside a flat, to babysit a full-grown Elder. I needed to prove to myself – and to my mother – that I could finish this mission successfully.

Clapp's response: "Nope. Talk to me later."

That tiresome "taking a nap" ritual would mark the start of each day. One morning, I apparently paced a step too close to his bed. He threw back the covers, lunged out of the bed and went to his bag. He produced a roll of industrial-strength silver duct tape and used it to lay down a line dividing our shared room. "This is my side, and that is your side," he said, pointing with the index finger of his one good hand.

Elder Clapp was interesting. He grew up on a farm near a small town in Idaho, which in my mind was charming, but in his mind meant we were natural-born adversaries right from the start. Wicked Metropolis vs. Wholesome Heartland.

But the differences didn't stop there. I was an advocate of nonviolence and he was into the ideology, into the distinct possibility of extreme violence. For him, violence was an inevitable, even necessary, part of human existence. Some people in this world seem always to teeter on the edge. Any small thing might trigger a tantrum and a bout of bloodshed, to dish out, to dispense, to punish with. And Clapp was one of them.

I found it ironic that a young man who was missing two and a half fingers on his most productive hand would carry nine knives on his person at all times – strapped to his chest, strapped to his arms, and strapped to his legs. By way of explanation, he would quote his favorite bit of Scripture, James 2:17: "Even so faith, if it hath not works, is dead, being alone."

"You've gotta have faith, Elder Moore, but you gotta back that faith up with works," he told me, patting his chest with a smile. People wouldn't be able to see them because they were concealed under his clothing, some in a homemade leather contraption with a strap that he'd grab with his teeth to cinch tight. They were strapped all over his body, these knives. Clapp would sharpen the knives regularly, with skill, concentration and precision, knives that could have no other purpose but to maim and to kill.

It was weirdly fascinating to watch Clapp emerge out of the bathroom from his morning bath to get ready for a day out, or lack thereof – the knives in question strapped onto his person, regardless. A ceremony of sorts: the putting on of the gloves, the strapping on of the knives, and, of course, the swinging of the nunchucks. That was Elder Clapp's exercise for the day.

He'd start by twirling his prized nunchucks rhythmically on his side of the room. But before long they would encroach on my side, coming closer and closer with each rotation. Clapp would place one foot in front of the other with a determined longing for balance on his face, and see how close he could get the damned things to my nose before I would duck. And then he'd put on that dopy, toothy grin.

Clapp seemed to like bicycles. Each of us had been assigned a bicycle to help us get around on our mission work. Clapp's bike became the focus of another of his obsessions. He would turn his bike upside down in the middle of the room, just over on his side of the strip of duct tape and meticulously lube the drive train. He didn't seem to care much about riding the damned thing, just lubing it, so that it would be in a perpetual state of readiness.

But one day Clapp agreed to use his bicycle for its intended purpose. I suggested that we "tract," or go house to house, in Bishopscourt, one of the richest suburbs of Cape Town. Bishopscourt is an enclave of stately mansions on manicured estates, surrounded by walls and elaborate gates and nestled on the back flank of Devil's Peak. We decided we'd see how the other half lives, and our bikes were the most efficient way to do it.

It was a breathtakingly beautiful day, but blazing hot. We rode our bicycles to Bishopscourt and began to ring bells at the gates to those magnificent homes, some with heavily thatched roofs reminiscent of Dutch colonial days, others modern structures of glass, steel and stone.

We stopped along our hilly route to take a breather and my eyes focused on Clapp's gloved right hand. I mustered the nerve to ask how it had happened. Surprisingly, Clapp smiled and said, "I was wondering when you were going to ask. Everybody, in time, eventually does." He'd been riding a tractor on the family farm, as a child, when it turned over, crushing his hand. I was about to ask how the knives fit into the equation, but he pedaled off.

In the course of several days, we tracted out a hundred or so mansions, but had precious little to show for it in the way of converts. We were invited to enter the gates only a handful of times – a couple times to talk to the help, who shared a kinship with us as members of a lower stratum of society. And sometimes we were buzzed through the gates by the ladies of the house, who seemed to think it was charming that we had come all the way from America to talk about our religion. But those ladies seemed to have more than religion on their minds. We'd be directed around to the back of the house and find an attractive woman lolling beside the pool. We'd be offered liquor, which we would politely decline, and then a cool drink, like we were children.

I can't tell you how wonderful it felt for a gate to open. That act of kindness by itself was enough to buoy one's spirits on a hot, unproductive day. But then to be offered a cool drink, with ice blocks, and to sit beside a sparkling pool and talk to an alluring woman wearing a swimsuit and a come-hither look. Jesus, it was too good to be true.

Dripping with sweat, I'd hoist the cool drink up to my face and press the crystal glass against my forehead in an effort to cool myself off, and sigh, and thank the ladies for their hospitality. One of them tried to show me inside but Clapp kicked me under the poolside table with a sideways grimace and I knew it wasn't on. That if I defied him and deviated from proper missionary conduct, in his company, the knives just might start flying.

Which meant a dip in the pool wasn't on either, as it might have been with Assante. Big smiles, these women had, but it was an effort in futility. They'd steer the chit-chat around to us, checking us out, twirling their hair with a single finger as they spoke, just considering the possibilities.

After one such interlude with Cape Town's upper crust, it was time to head back to Plumstead. It was quite a schlep to pedal up to Bishopscourt, but what a pleasure it was to ride back down to low-lying Plumstead. Our shirts, sweat-soaked in the early summer heat, flapped in the wind as we raced down the mountainside. Clapp would go like the devil on his well-lubed mountain bike, and I would try my best to keep him in sight. On this day, I had a flat and my chain came off. "I've got a flat!" I yelled to Clapp, skidding my bike to a halt. "I've got a flat!"

Now back when I was a kid, my dad's advice in such a situation was to go to the nearest bike shop and pay to have the flat and the chain fixed. That's what such shops are for.

So when Clapp doubled back and I proposed this idea, he blew his top and began to berate me, screaming at the top of his lungs, using all the lung power at his disposal. We were outside a Cape Dutch house, with a thatched roof. Members of the household peered out the front windows and the armed guards looked on from their guard shack, wondering what the commotion was about. "This is totally wrong!" Clapp screamed at me, inches from my face. "You have to take *possession* and you have to take *responsibility* for your own bicycle! And you have to *know* how to change a tire! And how to put the damned chain back on!"

He flipped my bike upside down in the middle of the tranquil, evergreen-lined street and expertly changed the inner tube as I looked on like an inept buffoon. He snatched a tool kit from his backpack and quickly got the chain back on. I tried to thank him, but he gave me an evil stare. And from that point on, he wouldn't speak. I realized, *OK, so where he comes from, you must have to do things by yourself.*

After that, our relationship worsened. We'd occasionally have appointments with prospective converts in Lower Wynberg or Plumstead, and we'd ride together to meet them. But by the time we'd finished our discussions about love and peace and happiness, the only words I could conjure in my own head were revulsion, disgust and hate.

I'm sure that these feelings were mutual because instead of riding back home together, we would pedal off in opposite directions. We'd usually get back to the flat at about the same time, and nobody was the wiser.

Then one day Clapp apparently decided he had had enough of this missionary business. He'd lie in bed and complain that he didn't feel well.

With partner Clapp in a self-imposed funk, I sought companionship with the other two missionaries who lived in the flat, W. and Holcomb, who'd been there the previous month with Assante.

Holcomb was tall and lanky with a conspicuous Adam's apple. He liked to sing, but was terrible at it. He had taken to heart a bit of advice from Assante about singing in the church choir: *If you can't sing well, sing loud.* And that he did in the choir, in the car, in the flat, wherever. He and his family must have sung Christmas carols together, and singing them to us most probably reminded him of home. The best part was that his singing was contagious. He'd start in on a song with his goofy grin, swinging his arms and snapping his fingers, and we'd soon start singing along.

W. was a natural leader who proved to be an inspiration to me. One night on our balcony, he told me: "Elder Moore, never compare yourself to another living soul, because when you do, you lose. You'll either place yourself above them or place yourself below them, and either way, you've already lost, because we're all individuals and all full of different talents and potential, and we have to encourage the good."

I thought at the time that he was trying to open my mind in regard to Clapp. But I realize now that he was talking about something far above my understanding.

* * *

One morning, Clapp, Holcomb, W. and I all fell sick at the same time, and we thought that it might be food poisoning.

We frequently were invited to dinner at the homes of local church members. The previous night we had dined with the Finnerans in a grand old dame of a house in Upper Wynberg. Harry Finneran was captain of a boat that hunted great white sharks. He was one hell of a big-hearted guy who sported an impressively burly beard. Harry had once been the bodyguard for the Mormon prophet, seer, and revelator, Spencer W. Kimball, on a trip to South Africa, and as such was the kind of guy who didn't mess around. Take one look about his house and you'd see that the sharks never stood a chance. The jaws of his prey were strewn throughout the house, on the walls, on the floor and on the rear balcony. We'd tiptoed barefoot through the shark jaws for the fun of it, both before and after our dinner, and now in retrospect, the entire enterprise felt dangerous. I'd never had fish paste before, and Harry and his brood were big on pate and all sorts of odd and delightful dishes pertaining to the sea, rustled up and served by the help. So we suspected that one of the Finnerans' seafood courses was to blame for our stomach troubles.

Holcomb and I went to the doctor and were surprised to find that it wasn't food poisoning after all, that we just had a mild case of the flu. After getting the OK from W., we decided to play a prank on Clapp.

Back at the flat, we found Clapp in bed. "All of us have food poisoning," we told him. We said the doctor had confirmed the diagnosis and that Clapp needed to report to the hospital within four hours to find out if he also had it. If so, we said, he would have to get a series of shots in his ass. We figured that the doctor would check him out, in the presence of W., our district leader, and give him a clean bill of health. He would then no longer have an excuse to malinger.

Although he had a phobia about doctors, and shots, Clapp went to the hospital with W. Holcomb and I were giddy when they departed but became increasingly fidgety as the time drew nigh for their return. We heard him before we saw him. Clapp stomped up the stairs, red in the face, and so angry that he was shaking. As he stormed into the flat, I could see the knives bulging off of his arms and his legs and his chest, tucked away inside of his white missionary shirt.

Rule No. 63: Be loyal to your companion.
Rule No. 65: Seek to be one in spirit and purpose
and help each other succeed.
Rule No. 109: Be courteous.

Clapp got right into my face, but he didn't scream, because he was gritting his teeth. With his jaw clenched, and in a thick

Idaho accent, this rich and storied and pastoral drawl, he in time spat out the words: "Elder Moore, one of us is going home in a pine box, and it *ain't* gonna be me."

When he advanced on me I was sure I'd had it, shaking in my shoes, fully expecting to be stabbed. Multiple times. But what I got was a warning – what amounted to a death threat. And then Clapp went back to bed.

* * *

The first person I ever saw killed was knifed to death on the Main Road of Plumstead, not far from our flat, while I was on missionary splits with W. So when Clapp threatened to kill me, I couldn't help but remember what being stabbed to death looked like. W. and I had been walking down the road when we saw two men scuffling across the street in a used car lot, shouting at each other in Afrikaans. One was a *bergie*, a term used to describe a subclass of homeless people who shelter in the forests at the base of Table Mountain. The other was a coloured. The *bergies* are fond of strong drink and are frequently inebriated. They're a fixture in Cape Town and locals tend to ignore them or laugh at their antics. When they get drunk in the street, some people think it's funny because they start to yell and throw things at each other. They generally don't attack whites and therefore are considered harmless. But this was different. W. and I stood motionless, like other pedestrians on the street, as the coloured man attacked the *bergie* amid the vehicles on the car lot. The bergie yelled in a repetitive plea, "*Nia*, God, *Nia!*" ("No, God, No!"), because the coloured man was stabbing him in the chest and the stomach, and he wouldn't stop. The coloured man kept thrusting a knife into the *bergie's* torso until his body crumpled to the ground and he was silent. He didn't even put up a fight, only begging to be spared. Nobody, including us, tried to intervene. We, like the other observers that day, just looked on in stunned silence. The killer ran off, and most of those who had stopped to gawk shook their heads in disbelief and continued on their way. A couple of onlookers ran to the man on the ground, who was bleeding all over the pavement,but he had been stabbed so many times it was a forgone conclusion that he was dead.

So when Clapp came bounding up the stairs to our flat after we'd played the practical joke on him, I was certain that my fate had been sealed, that Clapp was going to stick me with his knives as the other elders looked on in abject horror, unable to move, unable to flinch, unable to save me. It was a genuine concern because Clapp was off his meds and completely unpredictable.

* * *

From that point on, W. would frequently partner with me in our mission work. "I don't care," said Holcomb, W.'s regular partner. "I can sit here with Clapp and do nothing." I would go with W. into his assigned territory, the privileged white areas of Constancia and Upper Constancia.

What a pleasant change from working with Clapp. W. was a philosopher of sorts. Once he stopped along the side of a road, gazed up at the clouds and remarked: "This must be what it's going to look like at Armageddon – a day just like today." A storm was brewing on the horizon, and the clouds were twirling themselves about, moody and ominous, but calm and relaxing at the same time. I stood there and stared at the sky for a good long time and nodded in agreement.

Sometimes, instead of bicycles, we'd use W.'s car, a perk of mission leaders. We'd ring the bells on gates and doors and hardly ever be let in. But it didn't matter. W. seemed never to get discouraged.

About this time, in the weekly letters that we were required to write to the mission president, I began asking to be formally assigned to a missionary who wanted to work. I didn't say that Clapp *wasn't* working, only that I'd love to be companions with someone who wanted to work. It didn't matter where. I'd be happy anywhere in the mission. I just needed to be working.

W. sympathized with my problems with Clapp and talked to the assistant presidents. The mission had two APs, one from North America and one South African. Hall had gone home and was replaced by a South African AP named Groenewald. Because of my letters to the president and W.'s intercession, I was to have a conversation with Groenewald – at which point I had been Clapp's companion for two months. During a missionary night out at the oldest Mormon church in South Africa, on Main Road in Mowbray, Groenewald came out onto the grass where I was standing, put his arm around my shoulder and told me of my impending transfer.

"Elder Moore, we know you've had one hell of a time," Groenewald said. "And we want to make it up to you. So you are not only going black, you are going with the hardest working missionary in the field. He's a personal friend of mine whom I would jump to be companions with, if I were only so lucky."

Groenewald told me that I would be mission companions with Elder Christiaan du Plessis in Mdantsane township in the tribal Ciskei and that I would depart with Elder Young the day after next. We were to drive together across the country in a new car that was needed in East London, in the Eastern Cape.

A cross-country road trip with my friend, Elder Young? A new assignment to labor in the black township with the hardest working missionary in the field, Christiaan du Plessis? This was the balance I was looking for. Groenewald asked half jokingly if I approved. I was utterly beside myself, too overcome with emotion to say a word. My knees buckled to the grass, in thanks to at last be set free.

BLACK ELDER

CHAPTER SIX

In the wee hours of the morning, I remember rolling along Oxford Street, the main drag of East London, the car window down and my head poked out. And looking up to the solitary statue of a Boer War soldier, up atop his horse, erected as a sentinel to the town; on guard, on standby, on watch, lit up with spotlights, casting long shadows up and onto the town's Victorian Renaissance style City Hall, just behind. The soldier striking a pose through a ghostly seaside fog that was rolling in against us, the sentry and grand edifice of yesteryear there one moment, and gone the next.

We'd motored through the Klein Karoo and over the Tsitskiamma Mountains, taking in the sights of the Garden Route – admiring the beaches, and the girls, from Knysna to St. Francis Bay – and up the Indian Ocean coast to East London. Young dropped me at du Plessis's flat in Quigney Beach at about 3 a.m. I went into the unlocked front entrance of the art-deco building and got into the ancient lift, which lurched upward, haphazardly stopping several times between floors.

I had called ahead from a public telephone box on Oxford Street, and du Plessis was waiting for me on his floor as I pulled my bags from the balky lift. Du Plessis was called a "black elder," so I was surprised to find that he was a white Afrikaner, sturdily built with a shock of disheveled red hair and a face full of freckles, gifts of the African sun. Reaching out to shake my hand, he put on his glasses to see me better in the dimly lit hallway.

"We don't use the lift," du Plessis said, reaching for one of my suitcases. "Nobody in the building does, and you probably shouldn't either."

The flat, known as a "granny flat" because of its open plan layout, was tiny but charming, lit by a single bedside lamp. As I entered, I realized a sleepover was in progress; two additional missionaries were stretched out on the floor deeply asleep. Du Plessis flipped off the light and climbed back into his bed, telling me we'd talk more in the morning. I felt around for my bed, just across the room, surprised that the elders on the floor had been kind enough to leave it empty for me.

First light, and the missionaries were up, wrangling breakfast, making small talk, boiling a pot of bush tea.

"He wakes!" cried Kilby, spotting me sitting up, wiping the sleep from my eyes. "Kilbs," as I'd soon learn to call him affectionately, strode over, hauled me out of bed with a powerful handshake and asked: "Do you take tea with your milk and sugar?"

Rooibos was one beverage we were allowed to drink. Joseph Smith's *The Word of Wisdom* prohibited alcohol and "hot drinks," taken to mean tea and coffee, which is probably why I had a taste for them all. But rooibos, or bush tea, doesn't include caffeine or tannin. And because it has been drunk in Southern Africa for generations and has become the unofficial national drink, rooibos was deemed an acceptable beverage for Latter-day Saints by the local powers that be.

Elders Kilby and Little both had an air of small-town naïveté that I liked immediately. It was perhaps a result of where they worked – the nearby sleepy dorp of King William's Town, along with neighboring Bisho, the capital of the Ciskei's puppet black government. They were curious about any and all news related to the Cape – who had been transferred and to where, what the latest group of sister missionaries looked like, and life in general outside the Eastern Cape.

I took a quick bath, combed my hair, rolled myself a spliff – but then looked into the mirror and thought better of it – and threw on my missionary uniform. Du Plessis was tapping his watch as I once did to urge Clapp to get a move on, and we were out the door. Places to go, people to meet.

Du Plessis was clearly older, probably in his mid-twenties, and all business. "Determined" is how I would best describe him – save for a smile he would occasionally flash. The moment I saw it, I knew he had a big heart and that his hard-ass façade was a clever show.

The King William's Town elders were in town for a district meeting. The lot of us formed the Ciskei District, with du Plessis as our leader. District meetings were held once a month at our church in East London to set goals, discuss progress and voice complaints. It was a weekday morning and we got to the church and set up shop in a side room.

I took a seat and tried to size up my new friends. Little was a Utah Mormon with rosy cheeks that gave the appearance of a constant blush. He kept his arms folded and didn't say much, keeping his thoughts very much to himself. His close-set eyes were his most noticeable feature, suggesting the distinct possibility of inbreeding via a probable polygamist family tree. While Kilby, hailing from Waukesha, Wisconsin, was a different kettle of fish altogether, big on dry humor, dripping with irony, heavy-handed with wit. And that was only his smile.

Our meetings traditionally began with a hymn. As I flipped through the Mormon hymnal, idly wondering which would be chosen, I was taken aback to hear the assembled white elders break into *Nkosi Sikelel' iAfrika*, the banned song of the African National Congress, widely known as the anthem of the anti-apartheid movement. The song, which means "Lord, Bless Africa" in Xhosa, is a lively tune, especially when one gets to the clicks in the Xhosa language. I just listened at first and then joined in the chorus. I sang along and raised my fist, along with the other missionaries that day, thinking, *I'm not sure if this is still banned, but I'm all in.*

Kilby had been assigned the "role play" section of the meeting, in which we were supposed to practice building "relationships of trust" in order to convert and baptize people. But he adjusted his lesson to practice how to get friends and family back home to send us more packages of goodies – homemade cookies, photos and presents, which he deemed necessary for good morale in a place like King William's Town.

During the complaints portion of the meeting, Kilby again raised his hand. He leaned back precariously in his chair, balancing on the back legs, and asked with what appeared to be genuine concern: "Du Plessis, ah, what do we do when a family in the church, a white family, will not wear their garments?" He was referring to church-endorsed underwear – tops and bottoms, like long johns – that the good people of the church are required to wear to keep safe and pure. They feature Mason-inspired symbols, embroidered over nipples and navel.

"Well, what do you mean?" du Plessis asked after puzzling over the question a moment. "Some people join the church and find that garments interfere with their skin, so they've got to be reminded it's possible to try out a different material. You've got your standard cotton, you've got mesh for the tropics, you've got a couple of other choices."

"Yes," Kilby agreed. "The thing is it's summer and, let's be honest, garments cover up too much, and it's quite possibly a little too hot. But the problem with the family is they not only don't wear their *garments*, they don't wear *anything*. I actually think they're nudists. The whole family walk around the house stark naked and have swim parties together with other like-minded enthusiasts, naturist families, naked. And every time we go to the house, they're naked: the mother, the father, the boy and the girl. Their family photo album is big on nakedness. Because they're all naked the whole time. And I was just curious what we should do because the father's actually the leader of the Mormon Church out in King, and it's supposed to be his job to make sure the faithful are wearing their magical underwear."

"Luckily," said du Plessis, bringing the meeting to a close with the semblance of a smile, "we don't have to worry about these kinds of problems in Mdantsane."

*　*　*

When I think of that first drive into Mdantsane, I picture a multitude in motion, our electric blue Corolla weaving through the throng along a dusty stretch of road just outside East London. We passed the black settlement of Duncan Village and then drove along a straightaway lined with eucalyptus trees, the dust wafting into our windows and the minibus taxis flying past even faster than our Corolla. The Toyota minibuses, known as "black taxis," were crammed with twenty-odd passengers, the women wearing brightly colored head wraps.

"Elder Moore," du Plessis said, glancing toward me

during the drive. "You want to be a black elder, be a black elder. And don't let anybody tell you otherwise."

He told me he'd spent his entire mission working with the blacks, even when he'd been assigned to a white area in Kwa-Zulu Natal. "The mission office assigned me to work in this one white area with a missionary named Elder White, and I said, 'Fine,' and collared my new companion, and together we turned and rode our bikes in the opposite direction, to the nearest black township, where we labored and baptized and had ourselves one hell of a *lekker* fine time."

Du Plessis smiled and laughed and looked over at me again. "This is your mission, Elder Moore. Don't you forget that."

I took to heart this advice from an Afrikaner liberal, a rare bird in white-ruled South Africa. Du Plessis knew how to get results, and not necessarily the results the church leadership pushed us to attain, such as baptisms. Du Plessis had his own goals and way of thinking. He was a leader whose first rule was not to follow, but to blaze his own trail.

I loved the simple things about the drive to Mdantsane: the Wilson-Rowntree sweets factory that would melt chocolate once a week, treating all of East London to the pleasing aroma of milk chocolate; how the early morning light would peek through translucent clouds or the tops of the trees along our way; how our windshield wipers would do battle with the dust kicked up from the road by every passing vehicle.

Every morning, riding along with du Plessis in the sweet, early morning air, under a sky that promised a *lekker* hot day, I was beside myself with joy, thinking: *How lucky am I to be in South Africa, to be in the Ciskei, to be working in a township.* It was just so damned exotic!

Upon our approach, we'd see the smoke from dozens of fires   for cooking or for warmth   curling into the sky. Then would come the smell. With our windows rolled down, we'd inhale the aroma of the fires lit in scattered rubbish bins. I loved that smell, because it meant we were nearly there. And then we'd make a sweeping left turn. There, just across the road, was the Jekwa Petrol Station, a few shops, and knots of township residents with hands stretched out toward the heat of the fires. Now we were in the township proper, the potholed road curving up into the rolling hills of the Eastern Cape.

Mdantsane, by official count, was home to about a half-million people on the books, but we knew the population was much larger – as many as two million, it was rumored. It was impossible to conduct a proper census in such a place, with people constantly moving in and out and scant records of births and deaths. The only semblance of order in Mdantsane was its division into zones – 1 to 17. The zones with the lowest numbers were the oldest. The first cinder-block homes in Zone 1 dated back to the early 1960s.

On my first day in Mdantsane, we drove inside quite a ways, past the landmark taxi rank at Zone 2, full of traders selling live chickens and fresh fruit, and then a bit further, past a burned-out Checkers store. Soon our Corolla rolled to a stop in front of the house of a church member.

As we got out and grabbed our backpacks from the boot, Elder du Plessis told me: "Elder Moore, we're going to walk. We're going to walk everywhere we go. We're not going home for lunch. We're not doing anything like that. We're going to stay out here and we're going to knock on doors."

The brilliant sun had risen high enough to banish the chill, and it was now becoming quite hot. It felt good to be in white shirtsleeves, khaki slacks and my scuffed Doc Martens, now making tracks in the dusty street.

It was difficult to keep up with du Plessis, who seemed quite determined to remain one step ahead of me. He didn't take any guff from me. He had no time for concessions to a newcomer, which is what I needed at that stage.

We established a routine, usually starting each morning with a visit to a squat cinder-block house painted aqua in contrast to the dry, cracked earth all about us. We'd lift the latch on the tin gate and knock at the front door of the home of Mr. Khwetshube and his family.

Homes in the township were often identical in layout and very small. But somehow they accommodated a lot of family members, an average of ten folks by my count, including a good number of small children. The one striking feature of most of the houses that I visited was that they were well looked after – somebody forever with a broom – in a state of perpetual cleanliness.

Such was the home Mr. Khwetshube, a man of about thirty, frail and hunched over. Du Plessis told me that Mr. Khwetshube had once been a successful breadwinner for his family, a bank manager who had been mugged and struck on the head with a stone one dark night on his way home from work. Together we'd sit down to read with Mr. Khwetshube, whose motor skills had been damaged but whose spirit remained strong. He would open a book and point to each successive word, sounding them out more clearly each time we visited.

"*There is a lovely road that runs from Ixopo into the hills,*" Mr. Khwetshube pronounced slowly, his family watching in hushed silence.

That first day he struggled with the opening sentence for a good half-hour. But he improved dramatically over the next month. Mr. Khwetshube's wife would stand behind him, her arm draped around him as he sat in a plush purple chair in the front room. She would smile, and we would smile as Mr. Khwetshube would concentrate on the text and sound out each syllable.

Sometimes we'd meet up with kids of the church for a pickup game of basketball, usually with a couple of twelve-year-olds named Tules and Oscar. Other times, we would pitch in and help with their families' gardens, or with the gardens of their friends and neighbors.

As one from the leafy suburbs of Los Angeles, where I had been used to comfort, money and privilege, I found it exhilarating to be transplanted out of my comfort zone – here in the Ciskei, with my hands in the dirt, tilling the soil, sprinkling water, sowing seeds. I'd kneel there in the dirt and look up at du Plessis, who in turn would look back and give me a nod of acceptance. That simple gesture meant the world to me.

"Where are we headed?" I asked du Plessis on one of my first days in the township as we walked along a hillside footpath, me struggling to keep up.

He slowed down, put his arm on my shoulder and told me about the township's only hospital – Cecilia Makiwane – and of how, at long last, he had gotten permission from the administrator to offer our services. The hospital was to be our new service project, and that's where we were headed.

When I was with du Plessis, I didn't have time to feel sorry for myself, to think much about my mother's death. And as I became more familiar with the township, and saw the abject poverty, along with the smiles of the people in spite of it, my personal problems paled by comparison. I'd sometimes think back to the advice given to me by W. in Cape Town:

"Never compare yourself to another living soul, because when you do, you lose. You'll either place yourself above them or place yourself below them, and either way, you've already lost, because we're all individuals and all full of different talents and potential, and we have to encourage the good."

How true that is.

Our initial work at Cecilia Makiwane was with HIV/AIDS patients, who came to be our friends. We talked with them, comforted them and, with the help of a public health poster provided by the hospital, explained to them what the disease was, how it was contracted and how important it was to explain all this to their loved ones. It was too bad that this information came too late to the patients we worked with.

We volunteered for the jobs that nobody else wanted, such as one long slog of a day washing cabinets and walls that had been splattered with some unidentified fluid, and attending to some of the hygienic needs of the patients.

Each ward had about fifty beds, twenty-five lined up along one side of the room and twenty-five on the other. The ward where we worked was for male patients, and their black legs stuck out beneath the white sheets all along the passageway through the ward. And here we were, two white blokes, dressed in white dress shirts and ties. We could see by the way the patients looked at us, with a kind of hushed reverence, that they thought we were doctors.

On one of our early days in the ward – No. 4, the tuberculosis unit, as I recall – we approached the first bed in the long line along the wall and closely examined a foot of one of the patients, poking out from the sheet. Everyone in the room went quiet, listening to find out what was about to happen to this patient. There are no secrets in a ward like this.

We held the man's foot, laid it back onto the bed and then stepped back, as if to confer. "We're ever so sorry," du Plessis said, just loud enough to be overheard, "but it has to come off."

And everybody in the room gasped: "*Yhuuu! Yhuuu!*" A chorus of "*Yhuuus!*" The patient with the problem covered his head with the sheet, and the others were obviously wondering: *What is it? Does the toe have to come off? The foot? The whole leg? What has to come off?*

We each reached into our trousers pockets and produced heavy-duty toenail clippers. We asked the man if it was OK to clip the huge, gnarly nail on his foot. He nodded in the affirmative, obviously relieved that he wasn't about to lose a whole toe, a foot, a leg.

The toenails of nearly all the men in the township were long, encrusted with dirt and grossly misshapen. They wore sandals and the roads were unpaved, dusty when the weather was dry and muddy in the rain.

The first toenail we examined had curled into the toe because it hadn't been clipped in a long while. As everybody looked on apprehensively, we held the foot tenderly and proceeded to clip away. By the time we finished, all of the patients were whooping with laughter. And then *everybody* wanted his toenails clipped.

It was a lesson in the power of human contact, the simple act of caring for a fellow creature. It struck me as something wonderful.

*   *   *

We lived between two worlds – between the blacks in Mdantsane and the privileged whites in East London. Those magical moments in the township faded with the light of the day as we drove back to the city, to our flat, to our own kind.

We were frequently invited to dine with Mormon families in East London, but du Plessis limited our dinner appointments to one a week, usually with one family of Afrikaners who were kind and – very important – knew how to cook. Their house on the outskirts of East London was along our daily route between the township and our flat.

Around the dinner table, family members would ask us about our backgrounds and our impressions of South Africa. The mother would tell us about the family's daily struggles, the children would boast of their successes in sports, and the husband would grumble about work at the plant and the prospect of being laid off.

The conversation would eventually turn to our current

place of work. "Surely, the moment you step into that township," the mother once said, with fear in her voice, "the blacks will kill you, will murder you? You're just dead is that not so?"

I looked to du Plessis and raised my eyebrows, as if to say: *We're sitting here, aren't we?*

The father leaned back, cut the chops on his plate, separating them from the peas, and scratched his head in preparation for the statement that I would hear what seemed like a million times from white members of the church in South Africa: "Elders, I'm not a *racist.*" The next word was always *but,* followed by something like: "The blacks breed too much," or, "They're born with pangas in their hands," or, "They're clearly animals and as such not quite the same."

"They breed like rabbits," one of the kids chimed in, giggling at the notion of taking part in an adult discussion, which was never a discussion. And we saw how prejudice, fear and misinformation were perpetuated.

In such conversations, family members would look to du Plessis, as a fellow South African, for affirmation of their views. And he'd smile this great smile that I read as *You've got no fucking idea,* but hold that thought back, and keep smiling. Until one particular night, having heard one racial slur too many, he became visibly perturbed and blurted out: "Elder Moore and I are actually going to be *moving* into the township as the first whites in the country to do so just as soon as we get clearance from the government."

We were drinking SodaStream Root Beer that night just after our supper, which was a real treat, still seated around the family's dinner table. And the root beer spurted out of the children's noses, not quite sure that they'd heard their compatriot, the Afrikaner, correctly.

"You're going to *move house* into the township?" the mother gasped. All of the family clasped their utensils and gave us looks of pseudo-grief, as if we were already dead.

I just about lost it.

"We are?" I asked du Plessis, slapping him on the back, quite certainly beside myself, unable to hold back from hooping and hollering, myself: *"Yee haw! Gee whiz! Man, almighty! This is gonna be just great!"*

*   *   *

During the next month, I heard various stories about du Plessis from different missionaries, always told with a tinge of awe. But never from du Plessis himself. If I'd ask him if they were true, he would just go quiet and smile a knowing smile.

Du Plessis, as it turned out, had been the stuff of local legend. When he was just a boy, so the stories went, he had rallied the workers on his family farm at Upington in the Northern Cape. He had figured out that the workers on the farm, whom he considered family, were being paid a pittance, and that wasn't right. So, at age eight, he organized a general strike against his *ouma*, or grandmother, to petition her – with a smile, it was said – for higher wages for the workers.

But the stories didn't stop there. During his time at the University of the Witwatersrand in Johannesburg, he started a student movement that spread to university campuses across the country. He met with Nelson Mandela and President F.W. de Klerk. He took up illegal residence in a squatter camp in the black township of Crossroads in Cape Town, living in a tent for two and a half weeks as a protest against the Group Areas Act.

And so on, leading up to my privileged association with him. He was fully engaged in a lifelong quest for justice, and his newest challenge – which I learned about for the first time around the white family's kitchen table – was not just a whim of a quixotic crusader. He had methodically thought it out and petitioned the local government of East London and the mission headquarters in Cape Town for permission to be one of the first white missionaries to live in a black township in South Africa following the lifting of the Group Areas Act. Du Plessis wouldn't take no for an answer until both institutions, probably out of weary exasperation, allowed his dream to become a reality.

The two of us were giddy with delight. But just as we were making final preparations, as it sometimes happens in this life, the ball dropped. Right as we were beginning the process of packing our bags to make the big move, and to make the dream so, the phone of our granny flat would ring late one particular evening, and du Plessis would pick it up, and listen to the voice on the other end, and proceed to throw the telephone across the room. Du Plessis was being transferred and our month of missionary companionship was over. The mission office, having taken note of du Plessis's leadership skills, was making him the new zone leader based in East London. Which meant, du Plessis, in time found the words to explain – it was up to me. I would have to soldier forth, undaunted. It would be left up to me to capitalize on the dream and to move both my new companion and myself forward. To take up residence in the township Mdantsane.

HOMELAND
OF GRACE

MIRACLE WORKER

CHAPTER SEVEN

News of the planned move reverberated throughout the mission. Elders, sisters and members of the church taking a moment to bend my ear, to echo advice, quite sure I'd been dealt a death sentence with news of these latest transfers.

"Make a list of everything you own," warned Elder Kloppers, a white South African friend based in East London. "Jot it all down and send the list to the mission office in Cape Town. Explain in no uncertain terms you expect them to reimburse you when it all goes missing. Which it immediately will! You mark my words!"

While my good friend Kilby was a bit more pragmatic, focusing on the topic of "death" in general, informing me with a wink and a smile that the only other white resident of Mdantsane – an Irish nun – had been beaten, burned and eaten by the locals in the 1950s. He gave me a note containing his latest literary effort, a cryptic poem titled

Dying World:

> *In 1840 a lone rider rides off and dies.*
> *In 1910 a carriage occupant rolls over a cliff and dies.*
> *In 1945 a war is on, a friend dies.*
> *In 1965 a riot breaks out, a cop hits her and she dies.*
> *In 1982 a drunk man runs over a family who all die.*
> *In 1992 I see the hazy shade of winter and wonder who dies.*
> *It's a dying world. Why do you think we all wear black?*

I thanked Kilbs for his concern and said I'd be just fine. It wasn't the move that worried me. Rather, what bothered me from the moment I heard of it was that Elder Clapp was on his way to the East London Zone, to take up residence in the city that I was leaving. Although we wouldn't be working together, we'd have to meet this very day – transfer day – and at all the meetings in months to come in the East London Zone. That was something I didn't like one bit. I was sure that I'd left that world of fear and intimidation in Cape Town, that by being assigned to a different region in what felt like a brave new world, I had been set free.

When he saw that I was brooding, du Plessis sat me down and tried to settle my nerves. He told me that people change, that I should look at the day's meet-and-greet with Clapp as a chance to make things right, to smile and to shake hands. Du Plessis had the audacity to suggest, with his winning trademark smile, that we might even become friends.

I knew differently. I had forgotten that feeling of dread that crept into my gut when Clapp came to mind. I had pushed him out of my memories. I knew that he despised me as I despised him.

Which is why, when we did lock eyes across the courtyard outside our little church on Belgravia Crescent, I was taken by surprise. I was all set to grimace, but he smiled – and I smiled back. Clapp strode up to me and grasped my hand.

His smile seemed sincere, and then he offered more than a handshake. He gave me a brotherly pat on the back, which morphed itself into a one-armed bear hug. As he did so, I noticed that the bulges on his chest seemed fewer than I remembered from our earlier time together.

"I'm sorry," Clapp told me. "I was a bit of an ass in Cape Town."

"No, I was an ass," I retorted.

We both knew we were right.

Clapp's smile had a calming effect on me. I could breathe again. With his arm still clasped around my back, I could hardly believe it when he confided: "I've thought a lot about it and am now practicing a little more *faith*. You see – I'm only carrying seven knives on my person these days, as opposed to nine."

We both laughed at this – an unexpected laugh. We shook hands again and promised to keep in touch. Clapp went in search of his new missionary companion and I continued to look for mine.

And then I saw him. His name was Zetzmann and he was incredibly tall and lanky, with Coke-bottle glasses perched on his nose. I was expecting a more commanding figure, someone with a bit more physical substance to accompany me into the township. But I was to be companions with a bloke who was all skin and bones – with no knives to compensate for his meek appearance.

I figured that if push came to shove, it would be up to me to defend the both of us. But, honestly, I didn't foresee such a circumstance. I had no fear, and was almost giddy with anticipation of the coming move.

Zetzmann and I closed the Quigney Beach flat, where missionaries had resided over the past twenty years, and made our way to Mdantsane, to the newest zone of the township, Zone 17.

The homes in Zone 17 were a bit more modern and

spacious than in the rest in the township. We followed local tradition and bolted the front door, entering the house through the back kitchen door. That led to an open-plan dining room and living room, and then to a hallway with doors to three small bedrooms. The road outside was unpaved, and clouds of dust would swirl up when the wind blew.

Just down the street lived friends and members of our church, Zenande Makeba and her two children, Andiswa and Oscar.

Before long everybody in the area knew who we were, and apparently approved, for folks would nod as we walked about on our business, shaking our hands as we went. *Umfundisi*, they called us – a term of respect. Like du Plessis, I insisted that we travel everywhere on foot, to be more like the people we came to serve.

Traveling around by car, we learned early on, put us on a plain above the local people and could even be dangerous. Once, in one of the rougher areas of the township, Zetzmann and I got ourselves into a bind, because we had the car. Zetzmann, as the district leader, was the designated driver. We had just gotten into the car, the engine idling, when a man approached and asked how he could join the church. Something about the guy triggered alarm bells in my head, but Zetzmann was more trusting. He launched into a list of things the man had to do. "First, you have to take the missionary lessons. Then, you have to come to church. Then …"

The man was half-listening, saying, "Yes, yes." But I could tell he wasn't the least bit interested, and that he was waving over some friends. As two young men ran up to our car from behind, I knew we were about to be jacked. I yelled at Zetzmann to step on it, and when he hesitated, I reached my leg over the center console and stepped hard on Zetzmann's foot as it hovered over the accelerator.

We lurched forward, out of reach of our would-be assailants.

But most of the time, our reception in Mdantsane was quite different. It must have been very amusing to the locals – a couple of white boys walking the back lanes of the township, shaking hands, African style, with everyone we encountered, trying out our Xhosa.

In the Xhosa culture, everyone is considered a brother or sister. *"Moloweni Sisis, Igama lam ngu Siyabonga,"* I'd say in greeting, introducing myself as Siyabonga. My companion, who over the course of several months, rotated from Elders Zetzmann to Marshall to Greenhorn, would introduce himself, and the locals would do the same, invariably asking, *"Uhlalaphi?"* ("Where do you live?").

When we pointed in the general direction of our little pink house in NU 17, they'd laugh and say in disbelief, *"Suka wena,"* which translates roughly as "Get out of here."

* * *

Sister Maureen Magwaca, the mother of twelve-year-old Tules, whom I played soccer with during my earlier visits to Mdantsane with du Plessis, gave us weekly lessons in Xhosa. She schooled us in the subtleties of the language with patience and a sweet smile. She told me from my first meeting with her that she was my new mother and that she cared deeply for me, her eyes wet with tears as she said it. I felt enveloped in love. Maureen and her husband, Bridgeman, and Tules, and the rest of the family were the genuine article. They were indeed my new family. And I cared for them as they cared for me.

In our Xhosa lessons, we started with simple phrases and the clicks. Xhosa has three clicks. The "c" was the most common and the easiest, articulated by placing the tongue at the back of the teeth and sucking in; "x" was the next most common, performed by making a click as if urging a horse forward. The "q" is by far the most demanding. When pronounced correctly, it sounds like a mini explosion in one's mouth, a loud popping noise.

I spent an hour every morning, using flashcards to practice words to try out on people that day. After I used a word, I'd move the flashcard from my right pants pocket to the left pocket.

"*Unjani, ndoda endala*" ("Greetings, old man"), I'd call out to a wizened old gent perched atop a small hill; "*Kunjani, ntombazana*" ("Hello, little girl") to a toddler playing beside her mother in the street; and "*Kudala ndakugqibela*" ("Long time no see") to a gaggle of boys who would often follow us around the central taxi rank.

The larger the lady in Mdantsane, it seemed, the louder her "q" click. As we knocked on doors in Zone 17, we met one very large lady who spoke with an explosive "q" click. Upon hearing our feeble "q" clicks, which we repeated to try to get just right, she laughed and told us we needed a lot of practice. Once we mastered the "q" click, she said, we could come back and meet her family.

I walked around the next couple of weeks practicing my "q" click, but it wasn't easy. It takes a lot of saliva to produce that loud popping noise just right, to get a loud a plentiful popping noise to materialize. But because the township was so hot and dusty, saliva was in short supply.

* * *

The bigger kids in our zone would dance the *toyi-toyi*, a warrior-like dance in which they carried placards and spears and jumped and jived as they paraded through the back roads of the township. They were frightening when we first saw them. They obviously meant business and we didn't know how they would react to us. Once as we were walking through Mdantsane carrying shovels, we came upon a group of kids headed toward us. Brandishing their spears and pumping their fists, they screamed in unison in defiance against the state and the status quo.

We turned around to walk in the opposite direction, pretending to be cool and collected, trying to hide our fear. But then we saw another group of protesters headed toward us, blocking our retreat. We had no choice but to step aside, pump our fists, thrust our shovels into the air and shout: *"Amandla ngawhethu! Amandla ngawhethu!"* ("Power to the people!").

And I meant it. For the first time in my life I felt that I had transcended the color barrier, that I was no longer white or brown or black, or any color that we tend to attach to fellow human beings. I was the brother of these kids, and they were my brothers and sisters. Many shook our hands as they passed, shouting encouragement for the struggle. The rest continued on their way, determination in their faces, their placards saying they would no longer live in submission. They weren't going to lie down and take it, as some of their parents had done. They were going to fight.

But not all of our encounters with groups of restive youths turned out as well. Once, as we were walking along the main road through the center of Mdantsane, we saw a group of boisterous young people on a dusty vacant lot. We waved to them, hoping that they would wave back. But what came instead was a volley of stones. As we hastily backed away with our backpacks held up to ward off the missiles, one of the rocks hit me smack on the side of the head. I stumbled upon contact and backpedaled and fell. My companion screamed something, but I couldn't hear because my ears were ringing from the impact of the stone. I felt for blood but didn't find any. I was only scraped and stunned. Worried that this situation could get a whole lot worse, I got to my feet and we scrambled toward safety as the rocks continued to hail down around us.

Living inside the township was sometimes a very precarious existence. We felt safe enough when we were with people we knew and trusted. Other times, the mood of the residents could change on a dime, and suddenly we felt very vulnerable. Once, I pulled back the curtains on the front window of our house and saw a white unmarked police vehicle just outside. Its doors were open and several white policemen were running alongside, pistols drawn and pointed upward, using the car as a shield. I watched in shock as one of them broke away, ran to the side of a neighboring house and then came back.

"Oh, shit!" I yelled as I pulled the curtains shut and told my companions to get down. Besides us – all four of the elders were at home that day – the only whites in our neighborhood were cops. And they were here to arrest and/or to shoot people. That didn't make us feel very secure. We locked the back kitchen door and telephoned our contact, a black church member who was a police detective. He advised us to stay indoors for the next couple of days.

But there was always a tension in the air of the township Mdantsane, something hanging in the balance of the place that one couldn't quite see as clearly as the protests or the police or the rocks, but was forever there, was tangible and real, that gave one a sickly feeling when one concentrated on it or tried to suss it about. To take out a knife to cut at it, to dissect it, to understand it.

* * *

The very fact that Zetzmann and I were allowed to move to Mdantsane signaled a significant shift in South Africa's racial policies. When I received my mission call in June 1991, my best friend, Steve Cypert, was also awaiting his call. Nobody in my class at Whittier High School was Mormon, so I had a different set of church friends. Steve went to El

Rancho High School in neighboring Pico Rivera, attended mostly by kids of Mexican heritage like Steve. Our families were close; I dated Steve's sister; and Steve and I shared our hopes and dreams, including the prospect of doing our missions together. But I was called to Cape Town and Steve to Cleveland. What I didn't know until I arrived in South Africa was that there was no prospect of Steve being called to work here. All the Mormon missionaries were white – pure-blooded, Anglo-Saxon white. That was a requirement of the apartheid government. Because Steve was Hispanic, he wouldn't have been allowed to live in the white areas. He would have been considered a "coloured," one of a lower tier in the rigid racial hierarchy. So for the South African government to allow me and Zetzmann to move into a black area was a pretty big deal. It marked a change in attitude and policy. And it wasn't long after – maybe six or seven months – that the first missionaries of color were assigned to our mission, for the simple reason that they could now live with us whites.

* * *

During my time in Mdantsane, I fell into a late-night routine of tiptoeing out of our little pink house in Zone 17 after Zetzmann had fallen asleep. It was easy to do, as we slept in different rooms. Four of us were living in the house by this time so I didn't feel guilty about leaving him behind. In fact, I looked forward to it – to the solidarity of some time alone for a smoke and a walk about our zone, to clear my head and to mellow myself out and to willfully flout the rules. I relished the noises of the night: the lilting singsong of the washer-woman who would soap up a sponge and cleanse her legs, dangling off her back porch; the pop, pop, pop of gunshots not too far away, whether fired in anger or celebration I could only guess; the breaking of glass, maybe a bottle or a window, it was hard to tell; the mournful tones of a pennywhistle, probably played by a boy lying in his bed or out on a stoop, unable to sleep; the random cries of infants, often the result of parents arguing; and a bit further off the catchy rhythms of Lucky Dube or Yvonne Chaka Chaka emanating from a muffled boombox in the local *shebeen*, an illicit speakeasy.

I would sometimes drop in. They knew who I was – one of those white boys who goes around knocking on people's doors. But they probably didn't expect to see me in a *shebeen* – a missionary who drinks beer and smokes pot. I liked to soak up the atmosphere, take part in the laughter and enjoy a bottle of Carling Black Label beer with these new friends outside my role as an *mfundisi*.

The *shebeens* held a special attraction for me, partly, I guess, because they were illegal establishments, were hotbeds of political activity and were great places to absorb the energy and culture of the people I was supposed to get to know and to work with.

One of the girls at our local *shebeen* seemed to take a special interest in me. As someone who had come all the way from America to live in her township, I apparently was as exotic a creature to her as she was to me. One night she sat down beside me in a corner of the *shebeen*, took me by the hands, looked into my eyes and smiled.

"You're not lost, are you," she said, more as a statement than a question.

"No," I said. "I feel as though I have finally home, as though I am found."

We gazed into each other's eyes for what seemed to be an eternity, squeezing each other's hands, until she leaned over the table and we kissed. I looked around a bit sheepishly wondering if I might be stoned on the spot by an angry boyfriend and his mates. But the other patrons seemed hardly to notice us. They were too busy juking and jiving to the Afro-pop sounds and hoisting big bottles of warm beer.

But patronizing the *shebeens* was not my only vice. For I'd likewise stumbled into the dead of the night routine of calling back to Los Angeles with an international calling card. About once a month or so, to touch base with Jackie Zambooka, my old schoolboy friend, to ask how things were going, to ask if he could conjure bygone memories of daily life back in our home city, to at times help transport my mind home. An addiction that was likewise strictly against our rules as missionaries.

One night in particular Jackie was a bit jumpy on the telephone, claiming the sky was full of smoke, that you couldn't see the sky. I asked what was happening and he was surprised I didn't know. It's all over the news, he said. Three white LA cops had been acquitted in the videotaped beating of a black man, Rodney King. The acquittals by a mostly white jury on April 29, 1992, triggered rioting in South Central LA and in other cities around the United States.

"It's the gangs gone wild, is what it is," Jackie said. "Whites, Mexicans and the blacks. You've got the serious gangs, but then you've got all the pseudo gangs, all the hangers-on like the kids and the wannabe bad asses, and they're turning this into an anti-cop free-for-all and they're running and looting and taking the city for a ride."

The next morning in Mdantsane, my companion and I were out for a walk when a group of young men loitering outside my favorite *shebeen* – a tin shack with tables and chairs decorated with beer bottle caps – called us over. We were reluctant at first, as the guys looked a bit shifty. But they were insistent and we walked up to them. One of them asked me to remind them where I was from. "I'm from LA," I said in Xhosa. They whistled through their teeth and each gave me a hug. My companion was leery because he didn't know these guys, but they had sympathetic smiles and he could see that they meant well.

There was a TV in the corner of the *shebeen* that occasionally would flicker to life. But the power was off on this particular day, so they took us to a neighboring shack where they produced a car battery. They lugged it back to the *shebeen* and hooked it up to the TV. With arms clasped around my shoulders, the young men pointed to the chaos on the television, playing out half a world away. They whistled again, and one said: "Whatever you do, LA man, promise us you will never go back. That place isn't safe."

What irony! Less than a year earlier, during the summer of 1991 after getting my call to South Africa, on account of the rioting and mayhem in the townships as reported in the press, it had been my friends in Los Angeles who had said the same thing about *this* place.

* * *

I was happy to live in a new world that was both familiar and distant. The good people of Mdantsane are about ninety percent Christian. But their Christianity is mixed with tribalism, meaning a whole lot of folks worship their ancestors. We'd see them in their ritual, the men, sitting round a big clay pot of *umqombothi*, the "magic African beer" in the words of a song by Yvonne Chaka Chaka. They'd be dressed in laborer blue overall outfits by night, passing the pot round and round the circle, taking long pulls, standing while reciting up into the sky what could only have been a conversation with the dead. And as a result, some of those spirits — so it was believed — tended to hang around on earth.

We knew this because one of our unofficial duties as *abafundisi* was to expel unwanted ghosts — sometimes benign, sometimes malevolent — from houses and, occasionally, the bodies of people.

Church members would come to us and say, "You've got to come, for there's something evil in our home that needs to be set loose." We'd look at each other, as if to say: Not again. At the house, we would perform a ritual that we called "dedicating the home," in essence a blessing of the home as a place of peace and safety for the family.

We were once led to a house where a young lady we knew from our church was sobbing uncontrollably. She was normally quiet and expressionless, but now she was a thing of wonder. Her sobbing would turn abruptly to hysterical laughter and then to a fit of giggles. The father implored us to do something to bring her back to her senses. We tried greeting her with big smiles, calling out her name, snapping fingers in front of her face – all to no effect. So we asked the father if we could give her a blessing.

"Please!" he said. He helped restrain her as I placed my left hand on her shoulder and right hand on her forehead. All the while we recited a prayer. She snarled resistance, but we completed the prayer and commanded the spirit to depart. Suddenly the young woman sat back, sweating and gasping with a look of bewilderment on her face, wondering what was going on and why we were there. We felt mightily bewildered ourselves. The father shook our hands as if we were miracle workers, and we shook his hand right back. I found myself asking, *Do I have some kind of power, or is this a figment of my imagination?*

A similar experience involved our friend Zenande Makeba. Early one morning she came banging on our front window. Zenande was normally gleeful and carefree, but when I pulled back the curtains I saw that she looked very serious and disturbed about something. I called my companion and we walked together down the dusty street to her house. There we found her children, Oscar and Andiswa, who immediately grabbed hold of her skirts. The front room was in turmoil, the chairs upended and hurled every which way. The clock was on the floor and the coffee table thrust into a corner, tilted to one side. It looked like one hell of a dust devil had whirled through the room.

What happened, we asked in astonishment. She said that lately this is how the front room appeared every morning. I looked to the kids for confirmation and they nodded in agreement.

"We clean the place up every morning," Zenande said, "and every night when we go to sleep, it's all right. But the moment the sun rises and we come out to see, the room is in shambles, just like this."

When we asked Zenande what she thought was causing these disturbances, her voice became painfully strained and full of fear. She spoke to us in a whisper, as if talking too loud just might bring on a rebuke from the otherworldly entity in question. The source of her house's trouble, she said, was a specter that she wanted us to cast out.

"At night when I sleep in the master bedroom with my husband," she said, "I awake in the dead of the night and I can feel her, before I open up my eyes.

"I look to the opposite side of the bed, and there's forever a shadow. It's a woman because the shadow has long hair. You can't see any flesh for she's only a phantom – a dark shadow. She stands across the bed from me with her hair drooping down, and she stares. She stands there and stares at my husband while he sleeps."

We helped straighten up the living room, but I didn't know exactly what to tell Zenande, except to offer a blessing for the house.

"In the name of the Melchizedek Priesthood, which we hold," I intoned, "we bless this house and all those who live here, and cast out any unwanted creatures, any shadows or apparitions who call this place home." My companion and I placed one hand on each other's shoulder and the other hand in the air. "Satan!" I shouted, now getting the hang of this exorcism business. "We command you to depart!"

But the very next evening, Zenande came again,

banging at our back door. She was shaking as she urged us to come quickly, saying there was trouble. We grabbed our scriptures, and she ran ahead of us down the street, barefoot and hoisting her skirts above the dust. When we entered the home, she said the problem was Sonny, her husband, that he was in the bathroom at the back of the house. We found him hunched over the toilet bowl, coughing up blood.

I knew the family well by this time and liked and respected Sonny, maybe because he *wasn't* a church member. Zenande's husband was what the locals called "a big man," a businessman who wore a suit and tie and had a reputation for drinking and carousing. As the senior missionary on the scene, it was my duty to give him a blessing to try to make him well. As the family gathered around in the master bedroom, I asked Sonny if he'd like a blessing. "Yes," he said, and I laid my hands on his head, closed my eyes and recited a prayer for the sick.

The wording of a Mormon prayer for the sick can take various forms – asking the Lord to cast out the deadly germs or to comfort the patient in their hour of need. But I didn't command him to get better, like I knew I was supposed to do. I didn't ask the Lord to take away the deadly germs or to even comfort him. What I did was to ask the Lord to bless and comfort Sonny's family, through him. I asked the Lord if he would let the family of this man be well, to be at peace, and to offer comfort in the trying times ahead.

Somebody had called a member of the extended family who had a car, and before long a late-model black Mercedes pulled up in front of the house. We took Sonny to Cecilia Makiwane Hospital, where he was admitted to the Intensive Care Unit, even though we, the family and the nurses who attended to him through the night, thought he'd be fine.

But he wasn't. Late the next morning, word reached us that Sonny Makeba had taken a turn for the worse and had died in hospital. We went back to the Makeba house and found the family in mourning. The furniture had been moved aside and blankets had been laid out all over the front room for the women mourners to prostrate themselves and to wail their lamentations, as is the custom.

As we stood around wondering how we might help, I looked out the window and saw Oscar in the street on his way home from school. Oscar was bigger than most twelve-year-olds in the township but a gentle soul. I told Zenande that Oscar was coming and we both realized that he didn't yet know of his father's death. She asked me to go outside to meet him and to break the news gently.

I ran to where he was and grasped onto him, to stop him from continuing forward, to stop his forward movement until I could tell him, until I could warn him. But the look on my face gave the game away and as I hugged him to hold him back, he held onto me and he screamed. He began to flail away at me with his clenched fists, and Jesus, could that kid hit. He was gasping for breath and I knew that his father meant everything to him, like my mother had meant everything to me, had meant the whole world. I told him he had to be strong for his mother, to be strong for his little sister. I turned him around on that long dusty road and we walked arm in arm and we talked for a good long while and when he was ready, we made our way back to the house. Where he stood at the entrance with a quivering lip, doing his damnedest to contain his grief as the entire family came and hugged him and for the longest time, refused to let him go.

FULL FRONTAL

CHAPTER EIGHT

Our grand master plan was of course to baptize people. In our living room. We'd hold what inevitably deteriorated into raucous baptismal services in a sky-blue portable plastic wading pool inside of our house. The baptisms would turn into raucous spectacles because they would attract a gaggle of gawkers who loved to see their neighbors dunked. A baptism usually attracted fifty to sixty witnesses, tightly crammed into our little pink house. It was free entertainment and nothing ever seemed to go according to plan.

There was something intensely gripping about these Sabbath Day rituals – a combination of the giddy anticipation of the spectators and the horrific hell on earth panic of their friends and family members about to be baptized.

Among the Xhosa, there was a widespread belief that even he smallest body of water was crawling with evil spirits. Water equaled uncertainty, danger and possibly death.

"*Yhuuu! Yhuuu!*" the people would cry, shaking their heads in refusal while clicking their tongues in rejection. "*Yhuuu! Yhuuu! The answer is no!*" The question having been: Wouldn't you like to be baptized, under water? Everyone seemed to have a story of an unfortunate friend or relative who had drowned in a river while being "saved." The irony was never lost, and the people didn't approve. Many township residents had never taken a bath in a tub, on purpose, opting instead for sponge baths, which we'd sometimes witness on the back stoops of houses.

So folks by and large didn't take kindly to the idea of *ukuphehlelela*, or baptism, by immersion. After long deliberation, a prospective convert might agree to a baptism only if a favorite missionary would administer the dunking, and if a friend could be inside the baptismal pool with the dunkee to hold their hand and to see them safely through.

Perhaps at this point I should say that Mormons, like the Xhosa, have a thing about water. As I mentioned in an earlier chapter, our missionary rulebook forbade us to swim for recreation in the sea, rivers or full-sized swimming pools because church leaders believed that bodies of water of any decent size are controlled by the Devil. The only time we got to swim – actually just splash around in the water – was in connection with baptismal services, which is why we looked forward to them. Along with the pre-baptismal ritual of filling the pool with a hose a couple of days previous to give it a wash and to test out the waters. Somebody had to clean it – a loophole we were quite sure the good Lord *and* Beelzebub would understand, even if our mission leaders wouldn't.

I recall with pleasure the innocence of those fleeting swims in the township, the solitary bliss of floating inside of our very own baptismal pool, daydreaming away the long hot afternoon as the world around us was enveloped in heat and dust.

Rule No. 6: Center your mind on your mission.
Rule No. 46: Do not engage in contact sports.
Rule No. 104: Respect the customs and cultures of those
who you are trying to convert to your own customs and culture.

Our baptism rituals would have been a lot easier if we simply poured water over the forehead as the Catholics do. But our little white rulebook clearly stated that both the baptizer and the one being baptized had to wear white baptismal clothing and that the immersion had to be total. If all of the limbs and hair didn't make it under the first time, we'd have to dunk again.

Sometimes people would need to be dunked up to ten times. And every time we'd try, the would-be baptismal recipient would become more and more frightened and as a reflex result their limbs would become increasingly rigid, their entire bodies thus all the harder to dunk, the onlookers laughing harder and with more enthusiasm with every failed attempt. Children would clap their hands with glee, members of the church, quite possibly recalling their own ordeal in the sacred waters would slap each other on the back, relatives of the recipient would look up toward the heavens, huddling together to pray.

We would sometimes loan our white baptismal trousers to fellow missionaries and to prospective converts who had agreed to be baptized. One Sunday I couldn't find mine. So I borrowed someone else's, took my place in the portable pool and began baptizing away. As I looked out toward the audience, the entire ensemble of fifty-odd onlookers were laughing louder than normal, I'm embarrassed to admit. And I was laughing right along with them, trying to submerge a certain young woman who simply refused to go under, meaning I had to go down and under the water with her, several times.

We assumed the position in the waters of the makeshift

baptismal font, holding each other by the wrists. And every time we'd re-emerge, I'd be told by a missionary spotter perched just outside the pool, that no, she hadn't gone completely under. So I would raise my right hand again as she clutched onto me for dear life and repeat: "Having been commissioned of Jesus Christ, I baptize you *again* in the name of the Father, and of the Son, and of the Holy Ghost."

I was trying to concentrate on getting her entire body under water, but let's be honest, we were both floundering. As she clung to me in fear, our bodies became more intertwined than was appropriate for a sacred ceremony. She was inadvertently rubbing up against me and there was a whole lot of full body contact. I realized, too late, that my nether region was responding. Might that have been the cause of the raucous laughter?

I will not disclose the young lady's name but she was extraordinarily beautiful. "You're doing just fine," I tried to reassure her after each failed dunking. "Just one more time."

She was latching herself onto me and I was clutching the girl right back, and using my chest to try to force her upper body under, my legs just below the water's surface simultaneously attempting to trip her up, to bring her down, again and again. From the moment we'd first laid eyes on each other we'd had a special bond. We'd hold hands and we'd smile as she'd taken the missionary lessons and progressed to the point of baptism. And now here we were, groping at each other in plain sight, still at it with our smiles and our holding of hands. In an attempt to subdue my carnal impulses, I tried to conjure an image of a smiling Jesus. But the white Jesus that I had grown up with as a kid had been displaced by a black Jesus, as seen on images of the Christ in the township. So the image was blurred as my mind was working overtime to push out any and all carnal desire, which wasn't appropriate behavior in a baptismal font, these rapacious desires that were consuming my head.

It was then that my friend and former missionary companion, Elder du Plessis, who was present at the ceremony, glared at me and, before the assembled multitude, delivered a harsh rebuke that everybody would have heard that day, that I can still hear to this very day. "Elder Moore, your *thing* is pointed in that direction," he said, motioning with his finger down low and to the left, "and everybody can see it!"

I looked up and everyone in the room was staring at my mid-section with their hands over their mouths. When I looked down I saw what they were gawking at. My tumescent penis, stretched out to one side under my borrowed baptismal garb, was as visible as if I were naked. Because, as it turned out, these borrowed white baptismal pants and matching, magical mesh garment underwear bottoms were totally transparent when they got wet.

Someone quickly gave me a towel. Deeply embarrassed, I stepped out of the pool and hurried down the hallway, accompanied by du Plessis.

"Elder Moore, you're supposed to be thinking about Christ and His plan for us," du Plessis admonished, stepping inside my bedroom and closing the door behind us, "about this young woman's eternal progression, about your own eternal progression."

I was peeling off my wet shirt and pants and under garments and reached for a fresh set of underwear but then reached again for the towel to first dry my hair.

"Du Plessis, is *Yesu Kristu* white or black, or do you reckon He just might be coloured?" I asked. I was trying to hurl what had just occurred out of my mind by changing the subject, and I was doing it badly, for the flush of embarrassment remained.

As a result of his silence and still folded arms I knew the previous conversation was still on the table, that he wasn't going to be swayed by my sidestep. One less experienced with du Plessis would think he was serious, the way he held a constant glare, his tongue often dripping in rebuke. But still I felt guilty, my face a hot crimson. As if to defend myself I told him I was concentrating on "love" and he smiled and I knew he knew exactly what I'd been thinking, as he solemnly shook his head.

I changed my tone, defeated, and asked if he thought everybody knew. I swear du Plessis was one of those all-knowing types, like a Buddah, who could sit cross-legged from somewhere just above and look down and see all and know all.

"Not to worry, Elder Moore," he said with a knowing smile. "Your secret's safe with me. No offense, but I don't think they caught you were semi-hard," now looking down to my shriveling member.

"None taken," I responded, quickly covering myself.

"It'd probably be a different story if you had a bigger *thing*," he said. "The people were just in shock to see a white *piel*, of any size, take center stage at a baptismal service."

* * *

We weren't supposed to have sex; that was likewise in the rulebook. No sleeping with women. No sleeping in the same bed as our male missionary companions, or with the female *mfundisikazi*, for that matter. No sex with ourselves. Masturbation was taboo, considered an abomination in the eyes of God, although I'm pretty sure that all of us indulged.

One would hear the words "I just can't stop" echoed from time to time from different corners of the mission. From those who were brave enough to speak out. For the rest of us, we wrote to the mission president in our obligatory weekly letters. We were supposed to confess if we had been unchaste in our thoughts or actions and to ask for forgiveness and a penance if we had. We found out later that President

Bingham didn't read our letters. That was the job of the "assistants to the president," missionaries just like us who skimmed our weekly missives in the mission office, reading aloud the good parts and chuckling as they pointed to an offender's photo on the wall. Passing our letters up the chain of command only if our self-proclaimed misdeeds had reached fever pitch, if they were deemed worthy of a reprimand from on high.

In all actuality we weren't supposed to have ever had sex before, with anybody. We were meant to be as clean and pure and chaste as the driven snow. We were meant to be virgins.

Like most mere mortals, I had broken that rule a long time back – in the company of a church "investigator," as it turned out. An investigator is what Mormons called someone who was interested in joining the church and was "investigating" its beliefs and practices. Which had made me feel extra guilty, because I'd been taught that sex outside marriage was wrong and I knew it was wrong. I was supposed to be a good example as a follower of the true faith of Jesus Christ. But this blonde girl (who called herself my girlfriend) began whispering into my ear in the sixth grade, basically begging for it. I'd already agreed to kisses at recess break, and before long we were playing footsie during our classes together. The foreplay would last the entire bloody day. We couldn't keep our feet and our hands and our lips off one another, and by the end of that first week, something had to give.

I knew she wanted more and it didn't take long before I relented, and broke down and abandoned my faith and listened – to the girl and to the odd and wondrous hormonal changes wreaking havoc within my body.

One day after school, the girl invited me to her home. She took me by the hand and led me upstairs to her bedroom, where she introduced me to a series of photographs of her family. She then slipped off her dress and lay down on the bed. I tried to help her with the clasp bits of her bra, but I was shaking with anticipation, mesmerized and frightened and utterly blown away, finding the prospect of undressing a half-naked girl more exciting than unwrapping a new packet of baseball cards. As I pulled off my T-shirt and was clumsily trying to get out of my shorts, she asked if I would mind if a friend watched. And, as if out of nowhere, another girl entered the room. I looked up and said, "Sure." But I was thinking: *What the fuck? What were the chances? Of all the girls in the sprawling seaside town of Seal Beach, why did it have to be her?* An investigator! She had been with her family at our church the past two Sundays, and I'd been specifically told by my Sunday School teacher to set a good example, to be a good little missionary for the church and to encourage her to join.

The girl had witnessed me singing that Mormon Primary tune *I Hope They Call Me on a Mission*: "When I have grown a foot or two. I hope by then I will be ready, to teach and preach and work as missionaries do."

The girl, whom I hardly knew, turned out to be a pretty astute observer – a witness to the proceedings at my church, to my make-out sessions at school and now to my first attempt at sex. I remember thinking that being naked on her girlfriend's bed was not the best advertisement for the would-be morally chaste. But I looked up and said hello, and she said hello. For a moment I thought she intended to join us, but she just stood there observing. So the girl and I got back to the business at hand, which was beginning to feel really great – until a door slammed shut downstairs and the three of us froze.

"Tell me that's not your dad," I whispered.

My girlfriend looked stunned, like she'd been caught with her finger in the jam jar, and then hissed from underneath me, "Neal, that's my father."

And I shook my head and said, "Oh, shoot!" For there

hadn't been time to get to the best part – and now I was totally screwed. My mind had been racing and now it was somehow moving faster. How to escape? How to get clean away? I took a peek out the back curtained window and asked if I should jump.

The two of us were frantically putting our clothes on, and my girlfriend brought her hands down slowly between us, as if to say, "Slow down. Think." And then she said, "No."

Together, the three of us started down the stairs, trying to look nonchalant. Which was when my eyes met the eyes of the father, a very large man with an impressively burly beard. He was a blue-collar worker, I'd immediately surmised. A tradesman with big and brawny hands. He looked as if he could pick me up, grab hold my scrawny neck and twist off my head as if he were killing a chicken. I was sure that he could read my thoughts – that I wasn't a model Mormon but a crimson-faced hypocrite and a thief and a liar who only moments before had been about to deflower his daughter. Expecting to be thrashed and thrown out of the house, I was taken aback – and very much relieved – when he asked if I'd like some lemonade, if we'd all like a glass of lemonade. And I realized that he saw me as a child, as one not yet a danger to his daughter.

Fast forward to Mdantsane. Seductive young women would frequently follow us around the township and hang around our house. As righteous young representatives of God, we didn't seek female companionship, but sometimes it was thrust upon us. One day as we were returning to our house, a group of young women snuck up behind us and rushed through the door into our living room before we could shut the iron grate intended to thwart intruders. One woman sat down on the sofa, crossed her bare legs seductively and said, "Bold and beautiful, *ne*?" smiling a wanton smile. It was a suggestive reference to herself and, apparently, to a recent episode of a popular American-made soap opera aired in South Africa, *The Bold and the Beautiful*, which sometimes included biracial relationships.

They were young and naïve and we were young and a lot more naïve. They were unaware that we were not allowed to satisfy them. That we were stuck in the rut of satisfying ourselves.

* * *

Baptisms, baptisms, baptisms. That was the mission's mantra. Mission leaders pushed us to get people baptized. Statistics, they called them, part of a numbers game in the work of salvation. We had to report how many hours per week we "tracted," how many people we contacted, how many Books of Mormon we gave away, how many people we baptized. I would have preferred to spend my entire time on mission working in people's gardens, reading Alan Paton's *Cry, the Beloved Country* or volunteering at Cecilia Makiwane Hospital. But I had to do what was expected, even if my heart wasn't always in it.

"*Molweni*, we are *abafundisi*, and we are here to share a message with you," was the lead-in to our spiel on Mormonism. Some missionaries used what they called the "three no" rule, meaning that a person being contacted would have to say no three times before these elders would take no for an answer. But du Plessis had taught me differently. "One no, Elder Moore," he said. "That is sufficient. A no means no and a yes means yes. As simple as that."

So when the people would say no, I'd ask if there was anything we could do for them, anything they needed. That usually prompted an invitation into the home to meet the family, which we would gladly accept and happily talk about anything but the gospel.

Before we could baptize someone, we had to lead the

prospective convert through a series of six "discussions," or lessons, on the basic tenets of Mormonism – all laid out in a set of colorful pamphlets. It was very difficult to get people to listen to us six times, coming into their houses to preach time after time, rambling on about our prophet, Joseph Smith, *Yesu Kristu* (Jesus Christ), *Thixo* (God) and *uMoya oyiNgcwele* (the Holy Ghost).

Our pitch was that we were spreading God's word, that we wanted to share it with those worthy of receiving it, that God wanted the good people of the township to stop drinking Joko, a strong, black South African tea, to stop conjuring spirits around traditional bowls of mead known as *iQhilika*, to stop worshipping ancestors and to stop playing soccer on Sundays. That was a short version of a much longer list of impermissible behavior in the sight of *our* God. And they would have to accept these strictures, as well as listen to our six discussions, in order to be baptized. That was a tall order.

The township's residents were mostly women, the elderly and children because many of the able-bodied men were away working in South Africa's mines. "All roads lead to Johannesburg," Alan Paton once said. And judging from my experience in the townships and rural areas of the Eastern Cape, he was right. The city was where the work was.

The women, the old folks and the children would open their doors to us and we would try to school them in our faith, although we were urged to focus our efforts on complete families, which we would occasionally stumble upon.

So it was that one sunny afternoon we knocked on the door of such a family. The wife came to the door with a smile that matched our own. I explained who we were and said at the outset that we would like to lead the family through a series of six discussions, just so she would know what she was getting the family into.

In previous meetings with contacts, we would usually just share one discussion about God and Jesus Christ and

His plan for us. But when we would ask if we could come back for a second discussion, the people would balk. So we came up with a different idea to try out on this family. We had made a fancy looking calendar with construction paper, with available dates for all six discussions.

"Yes, my family would really enjoy these discussions," the wife said, nodding and smiling. "That would be wonderful."

My companion and I looked at each other, both thinking: *Damn, these calendars are a stroke of genius.* So we penciled in a first discussion for six that very evening.

We were excited. We went home and polished our shoes. Shortly before the appointed time, we walked back to the house in the middle of the township.

The wife answered our knock on the door, introduced us to her husband and invited us in. The little yard just outside was well tended and the interior of the home was spotless signs of a stable family. The front room was furnished with a colorful plush sofa and a set of comfortable-looking wooden chairs with big armrests. In the corner was a television, which we guessed was always on because everybody ignored it.

We asked if we could sit down and they said yes. We asked if we could switch off the TV and they said yes. Normally, at this point in the conversation, we'd say, "*Singa cima umntwana?*" meaning, "Can we turn off the baby?" That was meant as a polite request to put an infant to bed or send the smaller children to another room to play, because crying babies and curious toddlers were invariably a distraction to the serious business of salvation. But the children we had seen grasping onto their mother's skirts earlier that day were not in the room, and once the television was switched off, the house was oddly quiet.

"We have put the children to sleep early, and it will just be the two of us," said the wife, who seemed to be a bit embarrassed.

"It's really a message for the whole family, but that's

OK, that's fine." So we launched into our first discussion, which essentially contains this message: "We believe in God, the Eternal Father; we believe in His Son, Jesus Christ; and we believe that He has a plan for us..."

About forty minutes later, after we had finished the discussion – which wasn't really a discussion as we did all the talking – the couple looked confused, sitting on the edge of their sofa, wringing their hands in what appeared to be intense confusion. It seemed that they were expecting something more.

We asked about scheduling a second discussion and the next four to complete the pre-baptismal process, if they wouldn't mind terribly. The husband glanced at his wife, and she leaned forward and said, "Yes, but when do we get to the part about the *sex* discussions. My husband and I are having problems in the bed, and we'd really like to talk to you about it."

My companion and I sat in awkward silence as we puzzled over the question. And then it all made sense: why the children weren't present, why the couple looked at us as if we were crazy. Because of a slight speech impediment that I've had since childhood – slurring my words together even when I haven't been drinking – the wife thought I had said *sex* instead of *six*. She apparently figured that God had sent a set of white, "virginal," teenaged missionaries all the way from America to the townships of South Africa to offer advice about sex to black people. She had obviously persuaded her husband to listen to us, as if we were experts. Which was about the time we realized that we would not be coming back for a second discussion.

PLAY HARDER

CHAPTER NINE

Transfers news, for better or worse, would keep us on our toes, would break up the monotony of our existence, the asseveration and promise of a new and unique twist in our world of mission life. And so it was that following a handful of months under Zetzmann's too-often straitlaced leadership, news that Young was being transferred into Mdantsane promised to shake everything up. And I couldn't have been happier.

We'd had the odd chance to hang about in the city and surrounds on my days away from the township, during the months we'd both labored in the East London Zone: gallivanting across the nearby Mpongo Game Reserve in search of wildlife with which to strike a pose; or out and onto one of our favorite excursions, adventuring our way along the East London breakwater during the Wild Coast's frequent periods of heavy swells.

The concept of breaking the rules, in general, was

frowned upon by most of our fellow missionaries (who were never shy to pick up the telephone to report on what they considered "un-missionary-like behavior"); but *straddling* the rules, when accomplished creatively, now this was different – feats of ingenuity that could be lifted up and discussed with smiles for weeks to come, mission-wide. For properly twisting the rules required imagination and cunning and daring. And Young was a master.

I remember the subtle hilarity of the two of us taking a walk on the seaward side of the breakwater while wearing full business suits, the Indian Ocean waves in totality drenching us, one after the next, breaking over us as we'd scream out in euphoria, clutching onto the steel stakes stuck into the huge cast-concrete *dolosse* that form the breakwater, nearly getting washed away. "If the waves do take you," a local fisherman warned, "they'll suck you back under the pylons and there's no ways you can escape, missionaries or no."

Which made it all the more exciting.

We cut one of these expeditions short because Young had an appointment at our East London meetinghouse on Belgravia Crescent, a tranquil side street just off the main drag of the city dotted with grotesquely twisted camel thorn trees. He was to meet with the assistants to the president and with President Bingham himself, who was on a tour of the mission.

Young walked into the meeting late, drenched from head to toe in a glistening mixture of seawater and sand. He nonchalantly took his place at the conference table before the mission leaders as if nothing were amiss, as if he couldn't comprehend why they were staring at him. They surely surmised that Young had broken the rules by swimming in the ocean. But to us, it was a matter of semantics. For we hadn't taken a swim in the ocean; the ocean had taken a swim all about us, for those moments in time, encapsulating us in the seawater proper. That was Young, one who didn't take the rules – or life in general – too seriously.

So Zetzmann was out and Young was in, and our new district leader's first order of business was to call a meeting in our little pink house in Mdantsane. Four of us attended, including Young, and we all dressed up in suits and ties for the occasion. Young wanted to rally the troops, set goals, lay out priorities and inspire us to greatness.

Young took our improvised podium of a couple of packing boxes lorded over by a tribal blanket by storm and spoke out to us with a commanding voice, complete with hand gestures, as if he were addressing the multitudes.

"A balance," Young preached. "This is that elusive plateau for which we are searching, for what the world wants, and yet rarely achieves. If we can find that – if we can achieve that balance – we are going to be effective."

It sounded bloody great, and we all nodded in agreement. Which spurred Young on to the meat of the message that would become his mantra during the short time we labored together.

"We are going to work hard," preached Young, his face serious and defiant, waiting a handful of beats before breaking into his telltale smile, the signature that we knew him by. "But make no mistake, we're going to play harder."

And our smiles brightened to equal his.

"Any suggestions on how we can strike this balance?" Young asked, his voice reverberating throughout the room but eliciting no responses. The query had been rhetorical, and we knew it. For Young was in his element and on a roll, his words rolling off his tongue like latter-day scripture.

"Less active work, this is where we need to place our greatest emphasis," championed Young. "Yes, we're going to work hard, but we're going to back up that work with fun. You see, it's all about a balance, out here on mission. This is what we're striving for. This is what we should set our minds to be about – because we're in this for the long haul.

"It's all well and good to baptize people," continued Young, now glancing over to our inflatable baptismal pool, "but if the people we convert stop coming out to church, where does that leave them? What does that say about us? What is the purpose? There is something more important than numbers. There's a family in East London right now, a less active family, who require companionship, who require a helping hand.

"And so we'll travel tonight out to Nahoon, to meet up with this family at the beach, after hours, after our day's work here in the township is complete. They can and will come back to the church. A whole lot of missionaries have tried to help them over the years. But we're going to be different. We're going to commit ourselves. We're not going to take no for an answer. For if it happens, if they do in fact return, it will be on our watch. It will be us who make it so."

Work hard; play harder.

I liked the simplicity of the motto. And to prepare for that first of many nights out, to earn our reward, we worked extra hard, knocking on more doors than usual throughout our community, wielding our shovels and weed cutters wherever needed, volunteering our help.

The drive out to the beach was doubly exciting as we were clearly breaking the rules, driving out of our assigned area by the light of the moon. It was a quiet drive as we reflected and didn't say a word. But it was okay because we were doing this for a purpose, we kept reminding ourselves. For a higher purpose than the rules could comprehend or define for us.

* * *

One would reside inside Mdantsane for weeks at a time and it was magic and yet unfamiliar and hot and forever dusty and as a result, be it winter or summer, one would find oneself on the odd occasion longing for a wet and cold treat. Dreaming of anything and everything wet as the dust blown world would push itself past, in unison with our feet on the go everywhere back township trails – the definition of desolate and dry. When we wrapped our heads around the possibility of access to the ocean and for an ice cream to boot it was hard to think of anything else. And Nahoon offered both: a hand-dipped chocolate ice cream cone and a swim in the sea.

A little Indian-run café not far from the beach sold vanilla and chocolate swirls on a sugar cone, and, for a couple of rands extra, a quick-drying chocolate shell. The café was on the side of a hill that slanted toward the ocean. The lady of the tuck shop, her hair and shoulder wrapped in a silk sari, would smile beautifully as she served us and we'd smile back. It wasn't long before a stop at the café was part of our nightly visits to the beach and to the home of a family that I will call the Wrights.

The nocturnal stroll along the beach, beneath the twinkling constellations of the Southern Hemisphere, was magical: the indigenous milkwood trees along the shore crawling with screeching monkeys; the delicious taste of ice cream on our lips; and the sound of the breakers, which sounded all the more sincere and organic in the evenings, void of the screams of kids and the warnings of lifeguards and the chit-chat of the beach-going layabouts by day.

By the light of the firmament, this was our ocean.

We'd park the car and walk along the seashore until we came to the mouth of the Nahoon River, where we'd meet up with the Wrights, a family of a single mother and a surfeit of lovely young daughters. They would already have the *braai* heating up, the *boerewors*, chops and hunks of chicken ready to throw on the grill and a pile of blankets to ward off the night chill.

One or two of us elders would strip to our shorts and

go for a swim, the dark waves jouncing us about under the star-studded sky. The ocean swells would lift us up and down again, and sometimes we'd catch one of the tamer waves and body-surf back to the shore. Then back to the fire to warm up and partake of a late supper.

I remember ducking beneath a blanket to get warm and have a private conversation with one of the girls. We were laughing at nothing in particular and rolling about a bit under the blanket as the girl's sisters waltzed past and giggled. Suddenly, it all seemed a bit too comfortable and I sat up. Wanting to be alone, I set out on a solitary stroll along the sand and back toward the breaking waves, now far out at low tide. I walked and I walked, far away from the family and my fellow missionaries, the sound of their chatter soon drowned out by the splash of the waves and the beating of my heart. I had been kicking the sand and looking up towards the heavens for a good half-hour, staring at the stars, when a voice just behind me gave me a start. "You're not going to find it," said the girl I had been flirting with, "what you're looking for."

I thought that only I had known what I'd been up to – scanning the heavens for a semblance of reason and memories of home. Reaching out to my departed brother and mother, seeking a reason for my being here, so very far away.

I'd been looking for the constellations I grew up with, the Big Dipper and the Little Dipper. With the night air so clear, it seemed as if I could reach up and touch the flickering orbs. But the Big Dipper and the Little Dipper – as well as my family – were not there. They were nowhere to be seen.

"We've got different constellations, silly – here in the Southern Hemisphere," the girl said, as if she could read my thoughts.

She draped her arms around me, for I was shaking and

didn't realize it. "I knew there was something odd about this," I said. And she reached out and clasped her hand around mine, straightened my index finger and pointed it toward the sky.

"This is the Lion and Small Lion," she instructed, our fingers pointing to the stellar outlines now visible to me. "And this is the Giraffe. And that, just over there, that is Mensa, what we call Table Mountain."

That's about right, isn't it? I thought. *The Mother City.*

I was transfixed. It may sound sappy. But that moment was profound. It was one of the few times on my mission when I felt grounded. I shook my head and said, "Oh, yeah, of course, you've got different constellations." And I understood.

It's said that the deep-red soil casts a spell on visitors to Southern Africa when they shift the granules of earth about in the palms of their hands. But I'd argue that for me it was the stars – the constellations above Nahoon Beach at night.

It was all right here: the beauty of the star-studded sky, the danger of the great white sharks lurking beneath those ocean swells, the delicious aroma of the *boerewors* on the *braai*, the touch of the girl – and the embrace of the firmament and the coast and the sea, all about us, every which way we looked.

Those marvelous evenings made it hard to stay focused on why we came out to Nahoon in the first place: to bring a family back into the church. The fact that we lived in Mdantsane didn't matter. Or that the Wrights were a family of females, or that they happened to be white, or that we didn't have the allotted kilometers needed to keep up our clandestine meetings with the girls. For we were engaged in something greater than all that: fellowshipping a family that had shown an interest in coming back to the church. And nothing was going to keep us from attaining our goal.

But the kilometers were a stumbling block. District

leaders like Elder Young were allowed to drive only 1,000 kilometers per month. Zone leaders were allowed 1,500 and assistants to the president got unlimited kilometers. Our flurry of extracurricular driving had effectively grounded us. Our monthly allotment of kilometers was nearly used up, in our very first week.

Rule No. 37: Do not go on road trips.
Rule No. 154: Use cars only within the assigned geographical area.
Rule No. 160: Do not tamper with the vehicle's odometer.

Back at the house, on a lazy afternoon not long after our previous visit to the Wrights, I borrowed Young's keys to the Corolla and took a spin around our block, backwards, just for the hell of it. And when I got back I ran into the house so excited I could hardly contain myself.

"Young, Young, Young," I yelled. "You're not going to believe this, but I've got the solution to our kilometer problem."

"Yeah?"

"Yeah, you see, when you drive the car in reverse, the kilometers come off. They go in reverse. They rewind. They go backwards."

I could hardly report this with a straight face, because the entire lot of us were feeling saddened and depressed and here I was bursting into laughter. Young thought I was fucking with him. But I wasn't. I wouldn't have believed it myself unless I had seen it happen. I don't believe this can be done with cars sold in America, which have safeguards to prevent odometer tampering. But for some reason it was happening with this Toyota Corolla, a model from 1989 or 1990. It was like a miracle from God – or a complete fluke.

"Come on, let me show you," I said to Young.

We got into the car, and I backed it around the block one

more time as quizzical neighbors puzzled over our strange behavior. Young peered at the odometer, saw that it was true and clapped me on the back. For every kilometer we drove the car in reverse, one less kilometer appeared on the car's dashboard display – click, click, click – the numbers rolling themselves back like dates in a scene out of *Back to the Future*.

Back at the house, Young rustled up a jack to lift the rear wheels off the ground, started the engine and put it in reverse, letting the wheels spin backward for a good long time. "This is a godsend," he proclaimed. "This is a revelation." Road trips to Nahoon Beach and the Wrights were again in our future.

* * *

One night we got the bright idea to TP the Wrights. TP-ing – flinging rolls of toilet paper into the trees in front of a house – is a common teenage prank in America, usually indicating the popularity of the teen who lives there. We bought a big package of toilet paper rolls, waited until well after dark and parked our car a couple blocks from the Wright house. We snuck up to the house and started hurling the rolls into the trees. Our rolls were sailing over trees and they were sailing over the Wright's house. Glorious and bewitching in the moonlight, the rolls sailed high and fast. All the lights of the neighborhood were out, which was good, although we almost wanted to get caught. For the girls to emerge and pin us down and tell us how naughty we were.

But it wasn't the girls who first protested our activity.

The Wrights lived on a cul-de-sac of three or four homes, all surrounded by huge *Celtis Africana*, white stinkwood trees. We were stumbling about in the dark, trying to stifle our guffaws amid the cacophony of crickets, cicadas and birds that serenade the night, when a neighbor suddenly emerged onto his front stoop and a loud blast rent the air. The geezer with a shotgun first fired into the air and then pointed his double-barreled stick of death toward us.

What the hell? I thought, as our minds tried to grasp the prospect of having our brains blown out.

"I'm going to kill you," the man shouted. "Prepare to die, you bloody Kaffirs, you worthless sons of bitches, coming out here in the dead of the night, giggling like school girls and throwing paper rolls all about."

The commotion brought Mrs. Wright out onto her porch, just in front of us. She fired her own volley of insults right back at the old man, screaming right back at him to put his goddamned gun back in his pants and not to shoot at the Americans, no matter how badly he wanted to. She shouted that we were on her property, not his, and that she'd gladly testify against him in court if he killed us.

The old geezer yelled back, not taking his eyes off us. He called us scoundrels, dead men standing in our boots and the worst type of whites he'd ever seen. He said he was going to shoot and to hell with the courts and the laws. This was South Africa after all, he said, and that he had a right to shoot trespassers in the dead of the night, and it didn't matter if they were Americans or Kaffirs or whites.

To which statement Mrs. Wright returned fire, screaming all the louder   that the blacks in the township treated us better than the whites in the city, that he was the worst neighbor in the history of neighbors and a shortsighted fool to boot and that everybody knew he was a miser and an imbecile but that he was about to make it worse.

This relationship obviously had some history.

After catching her breath, Mrs. Wright continued her tirade. She and the whole neighborhood, she said, the whole city for that matter, would dance on his grave after he was hung by the neck till he was dead, after he'd effectively killed himself. Because he'd be sentenced to death for killing Americans. And didn't he know the FBI would come knocking on his door, that he'd be an international fool if he opened fire on us? That newspapers around the world would declare him a blockhead, which fact the whole town already knew?

They kept yelling back and forth, insulting each other with all of the lungpower at their disposal, airing grievances piled up over the years. Finally, the man turned to Mrs. Wright, shook his head and fired his shotgun into the air one last time before stepping back into his house and slamming the door.

We weren't laughing anymore. We didn't think we could ever laugh again.

"Quick, quick," Mrs. Wright said, waving us into the house. "That man is crazy, and you're damned lucky he didn't kill you."

And we knew it was true.

"What the *fuck* were you thinking?" she queried, telling us we were lucky that all her neighbors hadn't come out onto their front stoops to shoot at us. Breaking the news that we were in fact the real idiots.

"You can't do that in South Africa. You can't come here in the middle of the night and start throwing things at houses."

"It was meant to be a compliment, it was meant to be a joke," one of us ventured. "This is what we do in America."

"Well in this country we don't think it's funny," she gasped, the wind visibly knocked out of her from all that yelling.

We nodded.

"Lesson learned," she resolved. "And no harm done."

Mrs. Wright was something of a firebrand in her own right, if you dared to step on the wrong side of her. She was tough as an old *veldskoen* and could swear like a sailor. We respected her for loads of reasons, one of which being that she and her girls were of 1820s Settler stock, descendants of one of the first white English families to establish farms in the Eastern Cape. She sat us down at her kitchen table that night and eventually smiled, her chin cupped in one hand. She had a pudgy face and a mole on her chin that in my mind defined her. She was a force to be reckoned with, and that night she was brimming with maternal instincts. She liked us, and, maybe, she had just saved our lives. That old coot wasn't bluffing, we all agreed. He had been itching to pull the trigger.

*　*　*

In subsequent weeks, we got together with the girls, again and again. And not long after, Elder Young's mission was abruptly ended. He was first pulled out of Mdantsane and then sent home early from South Africa.

There had been a conference in East London for two zones, East London and Queenstown, which included all of the Ciskei and the Transkei. The three-day event brought together missionaries from the outlying regions – Mdantsane, King William's Town, Queenstown and Umtata – as well as East London proper. While the leaders attended a confab, President Bingham conducted interviews of worthiness with all of us. Then came the main event, the zone conference, where we were taught from on high how to be good missionaries. But the highlight, which we looked forward to most, was a party the night before the conference at the beach hotel where President Bingham and his wife were staying. We sang songs, enjoyed Sister Bingham's famous banana bread and got to socialize with friends from the far reaches of the mission. Usually during such events, the missionaries from outlying areas would bunk with the missionaries in the city, East London. But in the middle of the party, our zone leader, Elder Zetzmann, announced that the Mdantsane elders (four of us, led by Young) would not be allowed to sleep in the city.

Zetzmann cited a lack of beds, which had never stopped us in the past. And because it took a good forty-five minutes to get back to our house on the far side of Mdantsane, we'd have to leave the fun early to make it home by our 9:30 p.m. curfew and lights out at 10:30. Young was incensed by the announcement. He rounded us Mdantsane elders up and we drove off, after letting Zetzmann know exactly how we felt.

Instead of heading home, we unanimously decided to drive to the Wrights, who lived not far from the hotel. The Wrights, who were all at home, greeted us warmly and sympathized when we told them that we, essentially, had been asked to leave the party.

Well, why don't we have our own party, they suggested. And that's what we did. We had music, an American movie on cable TV and the girls beside us on the sofa – all strictly against the rules. We enjoyed ourselves so much that we lost track of the time.

Around midnight, we couldn't face the prospect of returning to our house in the township. So we stayed the night.

At first light, we were up and feeling a bit guilty. We hightailed it back to Mdantsane to shower and shave and change into our best missionary duds for the conference that day in East London.

But when we pulled up to our house in NU 17, we saw that a mission car was parked out front, occupied by two missionaries, the assistants to the president. They glared at us as our Corolla rolled to a stop. We had been caught red-handed; it was apparent that we'd been out all night. Our hair was mussed up and our clothes were disheveled. One look at our eyes, and it was apparent that we had slept precious little.

The assistants said they had come unannounced to retrieve a flip chart and leadership notes that they'd left in the boot of our car the previous day, during an exchange with Young, materials they needed for an early-morning leadership meeting in the city. But they had a question for us. "Where have you been?" one of them asked, neither of them smiling. Guilt was written all over our sleepy faces, and the assistants to the president knew the answer before they asked it. The Wrights were known to anyone who had served in East London as a family that liked to have a good time.

Young, as our district leader, immediately assumed all the blame, saying it was his idea and that we had protested, but he had retained the keys to the car.

"We've been out for the night after we were kicked out of the Binghams' party," he said.

"Where did you go?"

No answer.

"Where have you been?"

"We slept over with a member family."

"With what member family?"

"With the Wrights."

Young was immediately "emergency transferred" out of our zone, down to Port Elizabeth. Elder Basjan, a South African, was transferred in as our new district leader.

But that didn't keep Young away.

He would phone me to let me know he was on his way, and we'd meet at a pre-determined spot in the township. Then he would take me and my companion to a rendezvous with the Wrights, who now were completely off limits.

Together, we'd go to Nahoon Beach or to more obscure Cove Rock, to swim and to party – regulations be damned.

Young timed his visits so that he wouldn't be around when the Port Elizabeth zone leaders phoned to get the weekly stats: the number of hours missionaries in his district had tracted, how many Books of Mormons they handed out, how many people they had converted, and so on. Once when he didn't answer because he was with the Wrights in East London, the Port Elizabeth zone leaders drove to his house.

When they didn't find his car, they quickly put two and two together and contacted the assistants to the president. The branch president, or leader of the church in East London, was dispatched to the Wright house where he found Young's Port Elizabeth-based car. He knocked on the door and delivered the curt message that President Bingham wanted a word.

Young was flown down to Cape Town and, according to the story that made the rounds of the mission, he was offered the choice of a stateside mission or to simply go home early, his mission incomplete.

He had let himself be caught, and probably he was relieved by it. He was fed up with all the inane rules and the hypocrisy, with the backbiting and gossip and the snitching by fellow missionaries to advance their own interests.

While Young was based in East London, if anything ever went wrong, if anyone was accused of wrongdoing, Young was the one who got the blame, even before the facts were fully known.

A church member might see a pair of missionaries at the beach or at the Mpongo Game Reserve on an off day and, perhaps not meaning any harm, mention it to the leader of the church in the city. Before long, word would spread among the missionaries that a certain pair of elders were seen breaking the rules, were out there having a whale of a good time. The fingers would inevitably point to Young. So he adapted his behavior so as not to disappoint.

"Some of the time, sure it's true," he told me, "I did it. But most of the time it wasn't me. There are a whole lot of missionaries in the East London Zone and I can't be everywhere at once. But if they're going to blame me for things I haven't even done, I might as well do them. I might as well enjoy the misdeed. I might as well take the credit and fulfill their expectations."

Young had been wrestling for some time with an internal

conflict. As a direct descendant of an early prophet of the church, much was expected of him. But he found that, in good conscience, he just couldn't deliver.

Once, when he was still working in East London, before being transferred to Mdantsane, he and I had both attended a "testimony" meeting — a time to stand up and "bare your testimony" that Jesus is the Christ, that God is the Eternal Father, that Joseph Smith was a true prophet who brought forth the true gospel of Jesus Christ in these latter days, etc., etc.

The impromptu, unofficial meeting was called on a rained-out P-Day, or preparation day, at the East London flat of a pair of missionaries. One after another, missionaries stood up and followed the script, adding how much they were enjoying their missions. By this stage I had stopped baring my testimony in public, and I noticed that Young didn't either. Then Young stood and, in a booming voice, declared: "Stop the rumors! Stop the rumors! Just bloody well stop the rumors! I've known a lot of good members of the church here in East London, who are not big on rumors. And I've known a *hell* of a lot of missionaries who are all big on rumors. And so I say again: Stop the rumors!"

Young sat down, and I stood up and said, "Amen!"

He was tired of the self-righteousness and the notion that because a missionary continuously knocks on doors he must be a fine example of what a missionary should be. A "tracting elder" is what these missionaries proudly called themselves, never mind that knocking on doors was one of the least productive ways to go about missionary work. Young was an excellent missionary and a fine role model in his own unique way, but the other missionaries just couldn't see it. The backbiting, finger-pointing and the holier-than-thou attitude of far too many missionaries in this zone had done the trick. They had turned Young into the troublemaker they all believed him to be. The rule breaker, the rule bender, the one with a family pedigree that they all envied because, in their minds, that placed him on a level closer to God. Which is why they couldn't swallow the fact that he did things his own way. That he thought for himself. That he led instead of blindly following.

By the time he was sent home, Young's departure was a commentary on the mission itself. On the rules, on the leadership, and on the widespread practice of tattling like a schoolchild on anyone who steps out of line, who is in search of something more.

When President Bingham came to our zone for a special meeting to deliver in person the news of Young's departure, he had tears in his eyes and it was difficult for him to speak. He choked back the tears and forced out the words. He had loved Young, a golden boy because of his lineage, but also because he saw his great potential.

"He could have done anything," President Bingham said. "He could have been the greatest leader this mission has ever seen, but for the fact that there were those amongst us who were too quick to point the finger, to lift the telephone receiver.

"What we have to do from this point forward is to be our brother's keeper," the president said, "not our brother's tattler. That means to love our brother, to council our brother, to believe in our brother. Not to point the finger and tattle on our brother.

"There is a line – in that the rules are quite clear," Bingham said. "And when you witness someone hovering on that line, potentially about to cross it, you speak to that person first. You don't pick up the telephone and speak to everybody else, or pick up the phone and attempt to speak to me. You're not meant to be your brother's tattler. You're meant to be your brother's keeper. And being your brother's keeper means you speak to them, you discuss with them in a spirit of love and humility, about the direction they are headed. And you attempt to steer them right, into making the correct choice."

Young had explained to Bingham why he had bent or broken the rules, why he had willfully become the hellion that many in the mission had pre-determined him to be. Bingham was a wise and learned man, and he understood. Young had explained that he was tired, and that it was his choice to go home early.

Bingham didn't say that the missionaries in the meeting room that day should be pointing their fingers at themselves. He didn't have to. It had been these missionaries who had sent Young packing. It had been their vindictiveness and their faux piety. The mission had failed him, and as I looked about the audience of elders and sisters that day, I didn't see a dry eye in the room.

The mission mourned the loss of Elder Young. He had been my friend but he had had an impact on many throughout the mission. The point was that all of us are fallible, that all of us are human.

As for that night with Young and the Wrights, when we'd been caught tossing toilet paper rolls into the trees, I saw something that had a lasting impact on me. For just inside the Wrights' front door, in the hallway off the living room that led to the bedrooms, was a collage of photographs of past missionaries who had likewise been taken into the family's confidence, who had been allowed to grace the family's front porch steps. And if Mrs. Wright liked them, actually be invited inside. Those missionaries she didn't like she'd send packing. "Get out! No, no, no, not you," she once told me she'd said. "Send somebody who can smile, somebody with a little soul."

What the vast majority of the missionaries up on the wall had in common was that we were starry-eyed, young and good-natured. I studied the wall that night and wasn't surprised to find multiple photos of Elders Young and

Assante and W. and Hall. A wall of leaders I admired and looked up to, captured here in freeze frame, captured here in time. A wall of the chosen.

I looked to the collage and back to my friends in the house late that night and saw that we and the elders in the snapshots all wore the same relaxed smile. It reminded me that, despite all the pressure to spread the good news of our faith, we could all go about it in our own different ways – and even have a little fun doing it.

HOMELAND
OF STRUGGLE

RACE RIOT

CHAPTER TEN

Umtata, capital of the old Transkei, was a hurly-burly of noise, color and raw energy. It assaulted the senses and made a mockery of any sense of order. Traffic was a snarled mess. Car horns honked incessantly. The streets were chockablock with trader stalls, scooters, trucks and cars, many of them triple-parked. Afro-pop music blared from boom boxes. And laws seemed to be only suggestions. The gritty city – ninety-seven percent black – brimmed with life, but reminders of death were ever present. On the pavement were fresh chalk outlines of the latest victims of stabbings or shootings, and the local people strolled past unflinchingly without so much as a second glance.

Those were my first impressions of the city of my new assignment, as one coming from a township where the pace was several strides slower.

I'd taken the drive from East London with Zed

Hargraves, a young American from Cochran, Georgia, who spoke with a somewhat strained smile in defiance to the glare from the sun, his speech slow and methodical and heavy-handed in a heady southern drawl. Hargraves was a fresh-faced Caucasian, but his features were rustic, weatherworn and true – an ode to the great outdoors, that face – and as he gazed about and took it all in, there wasn't a flinch of fear in his demeanor.

"Have you ever seen anything like it, boy?" Hargraves asked, taking in the chaos all around us. "Anything in your entire life?"

I liked Hargraves. And I loved Umtata.

There was a frontier lawlessness about the city, in part, I imagined, because of the Transkei's nominal independence. The territory's leader, General Bantu Holomisa, was no stooge like the ruler of the Ciskei Bantustan to the southwest. He was a former soldier and firebrand politician who regularly spoke out against South Africa's white-minority regime. Nelson Mandela would eventually tap him as deputy minister for the environment and tourism after Mandela won the presidency in 1994.

Umtata boasted remnants of its colonial past, such as the neoclassical City Hall and other sandstone buildings of the early twentieth century, standing amid more modern structures. It was clearly a city on the rise, if somewhat haltingly. A gigantic skyscraper of steel and glass, intended to house the Transkei Development Authority, was currently empty, we were told, because there was no money to outfit it.

We tried to pull into a petrol station to top up our tank, but were kept from entering by striking pump attendants, who waved away would-be customers.

So we drove to our new home, which I loved at first sight. The missionary house was a big, cheery single-story building that hinted of a former grandeur typical of the neighborhood. The property, ringed by a chain-link fence, was in the Norwood District, a couple blocks from the city center, just over a small bridge that spanned the Umtata River.

We'd rung ahead and so the elders were waiting at the gate to meet us, swinging it open upon our arrival as we motored our way through. I noticed a Rottweiler mix who shadowed the car until we pulled to a stop, tackling me to the ground as I foolishly opened my door and got out. There was something overtly jovial about our dog as we rolled about in the dust – a nervous laughter escaping my lips as I realized she wasn't so much of a biter as a licker, the heavy breathing of a Rott sounding something like unto a growl. "There's a clever girl," I said a bit nervously, wanting to stay on good terms with such a formidable creature. "What a clever girl!"

"Don't worry, she's completely harmless, our Gadianton," said the taller and lankier of the two missionaries. He introduced himself with a mischievous grin as Elder Parkin, reaching down to shake my hand and pull me to my feet.

"And my name is Stamps," said the other, bigger missionary, now taking his turn to size me up while shaking hands. "It's her job to keep the robbers out," Stamps said, nodding in the direction of the dog, whose name referred to a band of robbers in the Book of Mormon. "Although she really prefers to sleep. We got robbed a couple of months back. The robbers broke the back window and made their way through the house and pillaged the place nice and thorough, and Gadianton just laid there in a deep sleep, quite contentedly curled up in her bed."

Parkin and Stamps were friendly and brimming with personality, not unlike Gadianton. Parkin was my new companion, a fellow native son of Southern California, from Costa Mesa, next to Newport Beach. From the moment we shook hands, we got on, as South Africans like to say, like a house on fire.

It didn't take long to notice that Parkin didn't always see eye to eye with our district leader, Stamps. They argued, usually good-naturedly, over every detail. Parkin would insist on something and Stamps would just smile and say, "Naa, we're going to do it my way." He had the girth and authority to prevail.

The next morning they argued about what we should wear for the day. Parkin didn't want to wear his white shirt and tie because it was a P-Day (a half-day off to prepare for the week to come). But Stamps insisted, telling him the rules said we should wear our "whites" in public, P-Day or not. And if Parkin didn't want to abide by the rules, he wouldn't be allowed in the car for the monthly trip to the city center to buy groceries. So Parkin threatened to ride his bike. They shouted back and forth like an old married couple. But, in the end, Parkin wrapped a tie around his neck and we drove off in Stamp's white Corolla, over the bridge that connected us to the city center.

We parked downtown on a leafy lane across the street from a United Bank. The bank was odd in that it had no bank tellers, only a handful of ATM machines inside a glass enclosure on a sidewalk.

Every month the mission office in Cape Town would deposit a certain amount of rand into our respective United Bank accounts. We tended to pool our money on the first day after transfers to buy enough food in bulk to last through the coming month. On this particular day, while standing in the long queues at the ATM machines, we were startled to hear a burst of gunfire, apparently from an automatic weapon. The gunfire was followed by a throng of screaming people running down the street in front of the ATM kiosk.

Rule No. 54: Do not handle firearms.
Rule No. 55: Do not handle explosives.

*Rule No. 35: Plan safe, wholesome, and uplifting
activities for preparation day.*

Gunfire in this part of the world is fairly common.
I had experienced several times the adrenalin rush prompted
by nearby gunfire as we visited with church members
in Mdantsane. The drill was to douse the lights and get
under the table. Then, when the gunfire abated, we'd turn
the lights back on and go about our business, laughing as
if nothing had happened. In Umtata, the night before, I had
noticed that on the side of our house that faced a tranquil
side street, one could occasionally hear a single gunshot,
probably because of the proximity of a *shebeen*/brothel and
other shady establishments. On the other side of the house,
the side that faced the city center, we would hear gunfire at
all hours of the night, with any unfortunate victims outlined
in chalk on the pavement, as I had seen upon my arrival in
Umtata. Guns were a part of everyday life. We didn't think
too much about it — unless the guns were pointed at us.

On this, my first full day in Umtata, the gunfire persisted
as townspeople screamed and ducked for cover behind
parked cars, holding tight to their handbags. The people in
the ATM queues with us howled in fear — "*Yhuuu! — Yhuuu!*" —
but kept their places in line, even as some of those running
down the street came into the bank kiosk and hid behind
the ATM machines.

Abruptly, the gunfire ceased, people stopped running
and things returned to normal — at least for a short time.
But it started up anew, and the same scene played out again —
people running en masse and taking cover wherever they
could find it.

At the Missionary Training Center in Provo, Utah, we
were told that when crowds of blacks run down a street
in South Africa it means that a riot is underway and that
we should leave the scene as quickly as possible. But now

that we had actually experienced such a situation, we took our cues from the locals. We were fearful only when they were, and lulled into a false sense of security when things quieted down.

We at last got to the front of the queue, withdrew our rand and headed back to the car. We noticed when we crossed the street that it was completely deserted, instead of teeming with people. It was strangely silent — no shouting, no car horns, no boom boxes. It was like a scene out of *The Twilight Zone* as we gazed up and down the thoroughfare, wondering where everyone had gone.

We jumped into the car and began to look for a parking space near the **SPAR** supermarket, where we were to do our monthly grocery shopping. There were no empty parking spots in front, so we drove around the corner. As we approached the intersection of Sutherland with Madeira Street, we encountered a crowd probably numbering in the thousands. Ours was the first in a row of cars trying to make a left turn onto Madeira. But with so many people crammed into the street, we were stuck. There we sat, surrounded by a mass of pedestrians, feeling very vulnerable. We saw that the crowd in front of us started to move swiftly towards the block to the left, where a petrol station was ablaze. We heard more automatic gunfire from the direction of the filling station, and people began to flee from it, running toward us, in the middle of the street and on both sidewalks. The crowd was a human tide in its surge and ebb, driven first by curiosity, and then by fear.

The only other white person we saw was running for his life. He was accompanied by a black man, who was holding the white man's hand and running with him down the sidewalk across the street from us. The mob was chasing them, hurling bottles, stones and bricks at close range. The man was hit, I believe multiple times, but he kept running. Just when the mob was about to catch him, another black man opened the door to his office, right across the street from us. The white man and the black man who had been running with him ran up the stairs to safety in the nick of time, as the man who provided refuge closed the door behind him.

That frightening scene, played out only meters away from us, made it painfully clear that we – four white males, wearing white shirts (at Stamps' insistence), in a white car stuck solid in the midst of a multitude of angry blacks – were in considerable danger. Our timing couldn't have been worse.

My first thought was that we roll down the windows and play it cool. *We're just out for a drive,* I thought we might say, *strictly observers. We're neutral. We're the good guys. We're Americans. We're your friends.*

In the midst of the mayhem, one black man on the sidewalk peered directly into our car for a full five seconds before turning away and looking toward the burning petrol station. We followed the man's gaze and saw a fire truck roll to a stop at the station. The firefighters prepared to unload their hoses to combat the blaze. But suddenly they jumped back onto the truck, and it sped away from the fire, toward us. As the fire engine approached, siren wailing, we saw why it hadn't stopped for long to deal with the fire. It was being chased by a white car occupied by two men, one of them firing shots at the truck from the passenger window. A fireman atop the truck threw himself flat onto a coil of hoses, trying to evade the gunfire. The truck turned onto the street where we were stuck and passed by the side of our car in the opposite direction, the white car still chasing it, and the gunman still shooting, now only a few feet away. His huge pistol was within arm's reach from me as he fired into the air. Briefly, he glared menacingly at me through our open window. That's when I lost it. I kicked the seat in front of me and yelled, "Goddammit, Stamps, step on it!" Both Parkin and I were now screaming, "Go! Go! Go!" We figured that the man with the gun would come back and deal with us.

Our car lurched forward, turning to the left, in the direction of the burning petrol station. The crowd parted as we bucked the tide of pedestrians. At the Total Fuel Center on Madeira near Sutherland, we saw an armored vehicle, which apparently was the source of the automatic weapons fire we had heard earlier. Black smoke billowed into the air as one of the petrol pumps burned. People began throwing stones at the petrol station as the crowd reached fever pitch. Black men in business suits stood in the middle of the street, gesturing with their hands and shouting in Xhosa at the onlookers to calm down.

They yelled at us, saying they wanted to have a word, and then they hopped onto the hood of our car as we inched through the crowd. Parkin yelled at Stamps to gun it, and the guys with the suits tumbled off the car into the crowd. When I saw these men, I thought at first they might be ANC leaders trying to control the situation, but I learned later that they might have been union representatives. No matter who they were, we weren't about to stop our car in the middle of an unruly, unpredictable crowd to have a chat.

We drove steadily through the mob without stopping. I recall looking back at the petrol station and thinking, *Damn, the fuel tanks could blow at any moment.*

But they didn't, and we turned again to the left and then to right and drove back across the bridge to Norwood.

At the house, we locked the gate and felt safer, at least for the time being. Parkin insisted that we park the car around the back so that it couldn't be seen from the street in front, and Stamps agreed. But Parkin also insisted that he be in charge of the car keys because Stamps wasn't very good at driving a standard transmission. If push came to shove, he reasoned, we might need to bust through the gates and get out of the city as quickly as possible without stalling in traffic. Parkin's father was a judge in Southern California and owned a stick-shift Porsche, which Parkin knew how to drive. I respected Parkin's thinking and the fact that Stamps agreed. Parkin was all about our personal safety, in a giddy, excitable way, which I had to admire. He wanted to take the legs off the tables to use as clubs should "the interesting people in the neighborhood" remember where four young whites lived and come knocking. But Stamps drew the line there, and the tables remained intact.

As we laid low at our house, the automatic gunfire still going on, Stamps got on the phone with our political contact in the city, Winston Dandala. Winston was a member of the church and affiliated with the local ANC. He told us to stay inside the house and that he would report back in fifteen minutes on what he found out. When he phoned back he explained to us the cause of all the turmoil in the city. The petrol station attendants, Winston said, had been on strike for the past couple of days. The white owner of the station had come to blows with the leader of the strikers, who were demanding higher wages. As the two men fought at the Total station on Madeira Street, near a popular fast-food eatery called Steers, a crowd gathered to cheer on the striker. The black picketer had been winning the fight, and the crowd had been jubilant – until the white man produced a pistol and shot the picketer point-blank in the head. The crowd immediately attacked the white man and his petrol station, throwing stones, cutting the fuel hoses and setting a pump alight. The police responded quickly, found where he had taken refuge from the mob and marched him in handcuffs the fifty or so meters around the corner to the Madeira Street police station.

The police had saved the man's life, but they couldn't save his petrol station. More and more angry protesters gathered around the station. The army deployed an armored personnel carrier and soldiers – who were shooting blanks, we were later told – to try to disperse the crowd. But that's when all hell broke loose.

Winston's call explaining all this was on speakerphone, and when he offered us the use of a 9mm pistol for protection, Parkin shouted, "Yes!" But Stamps said no, which didn't go down well with Parkin.

Winston ordered us to stay inside the house during the coming week. Members of the church rallied around us, delivering the groceries that we were unable to collect ourselves on my first full day in the Transkei.

The next day President Bingham called from Cape Town to check on us. He had a newspaper in front of him as he spoke and asked where we had been between 1 and 2 o'clock on the day of the riot. Right smack dab in the middle of it, we told him, but we had made it out safely. He told us to stay put in the house and keep him updated.

Within three days, Parkin and I were going stir crazy. So we decided to go out onto the street for some exercise. I liked to run in the mornings and Parkin liked to ride his mountain bike. We had made it about five or six houses down the street when a man in a Kombi rounded the corner and saw us. He accelerated and pointed the van directly at us. We only just managed to hop out of the way as he sped past, missing us by inches.

With that, Parkin and I decided that it would be prudent to heed Winston's advice and stay in the house.

APLA

CHAPTER ELEVEN

I was pleased to learn that my assigned bicycle was inoperable. But to seal the deal, I sabotaged it further. Which meant that Parkin and I had to walk. Once the violence that marked my first week in Umtata had calmed down and we got the "all clear," Parkin and I decided that we had to be outdoors. We forced ourselves to get up early and trek to a tracting location far across the city. We came home at night only after a long day's work – no coming home for lunch, no afternoon naps – following the example of Elder du Plessis: "Spend the whole day out in service of the people."

The now-gone elders who had most recently lived in Umtata and worked with Parkin and Stamps were known for their laziness, preferring to sleep late into the morning and take afternoon naps rather than trudge about knocking on doors. And I didn't want to continue in their tradition. It wasn't about piling up enviable statistics to be reported to the higher-ups or about being considered good "tracting elders." It was about just being outdoors, with the local people, volunteering our time and energy. When I suggested this strategy to Parkin, he was quick to agree. He didn't even mind that I had sabotaged my bike. Together, we had a really fine time, walking to our area, spending the entire day out of doors, and come the night, long after dark, walking our way home.

On our long walks home, we'd often fall into conversation about our respective lives back in Southern California. We both loved vintage cars. Parkin's dad's Porsche was a vintage 911 model and one of my friends had owned a classic Corvette. So we'd often argue about the comparative virtues of each machine and describe in glorious detail the exhilarating feeling of actually driving them.

Although we both appreciated Porsches and Corvettes, we settled on the first-generation Ford Mustang – 1964 to 1973 – as the ultimate symbol of Americana and the car we most lusted after. We especially loved the 1967 Mustang GT Fastback. So, on a whim, we decided to work sixty-seven hours each week, and that's the number we started turning in to our superiors. We were required to work fifty-five hours, but sixty-seven was our target, in tribute to our favorite car.

Our weekly hours were the one statistic we could control and we chose to focus on this because together we could choose the definition of "work" that would make our numbers so. We could have easily worked more, but we'd cut ourselves off towards the end of the week to turn in a secret code of a stat that only we could smile at, that we could be proud of.

"OK, how many hours this week?" Stamps would ask. And we would say: "The '67 Mustang GT Fastback this week. But next week it might be the '68 Mustang GT-390 Bullitt, or the '69 Mustang Boss 429. We'll have to wait and see."

We could hardly say this with a straight face. The

numbers would have been unbelievable, save for the fact that Stamps could verify them, knowing full well the time we were out in the field.

We joked about it, but actually we were pushing the boundaries of what we thought a missionary could be – out with the people, with no other care but to help our fellow human beings. And I must say, the two of us mutually noted, that working hard felt good. We thought about some of our contemporaries back in Southern California, absorbed with fraternities and sororities and trying to get the most fun out of college life, and here we were trying to buck that trend, concentrating on others.

But good statistics led to leadership, and within four weeks of arriving in Umtata, I was christened the new district leader. Stamps was transferred out, and the keys to the Corolla were handed over to me. Which I didn't want. That hadn't been a part of the plan.

* * *

I loved to run, and now that the racial turmoil in the city had blown over – we believed – we could get out of the house and run again. Hargraves was my new companion and a hell of a good sport. Together we'd run for miles in our rambles throughout the city.

We'd be up at first light, pulling up the socks and lacing the running shoes. Out the front door, out the front gate, onto the street. Breathing in the morning air, sweet and crisp. Houses still dark, only the porch lights still on. There was an ephemeral quality to these early morning runs – the brilliant early light reflecting off the buildings in our neighborhood, the city still half asleep, slowly awakening and chugging to life.

We'd greet the day laborers, usually women, who walked down our lane two or three at a time, with bundles of firewood perched on their heads. They smiled jovially, from the heart, and we returned the smiles with a greeting in Xhosa: *Molweni, bafazi.*

While some neighbors were still asleep or just climbing out of bed, others were about to head for work – an office worker warming his car's balky engine, a schoolteacher packing books into the boot of her sedan.

Norwood, our neighborhood, was very diverse, its occupants ranging from us, white American *bafundisi*, to the good-time ladies of the whorehouse cum *shebeen* just across the street. The ladies would lounge on their stoop and greet the steady stream of johns who came to buy their favors. They would wave at us whenever we passed, catching us in a blush and forcing us to wave back.

Our street was occupied mostly by families. And as we trotted along it in the mornings, toward the bridge into the city center, we wanted to be part of their world, to blend into the life of the city, as much as was possible for young white Americans surrounded by black Xhosa. The city's streets were quiet in the early morning hours, but the signs of a nation embroiled in violence were ubiquitous. Nearly every morning, we would see new chalk outlines on the pavement, drawn by the police around the corpses of those not fortunate enough to survive the night, arms and legs bent at unnatural angles in the moment of their demise. Many of the violent deaths in South Africa at this time were a result of the blacks' struggle against apartheid. But these memorialized in chalk on a gritty pavement were usually a byproduct of a culture of lawlessness that prevailed in Umtata in the early 1990s.

As we lay in our beds in our house at night, doors locked and Gadianton on duty, we were surrounded by the sound of gunfire – single shots as well as quick bursts from semiautomatic or fully automatic weapons.

Aside from the gunfire associated with robbery and murder, some of the gunplay had political overtones. Umtata was the home base of the armed wing of the hardline Pan African Congress, known as the Azanian People's Liberation Army (APLA). APLA members would use spray paint to tag the walls of downtown buildings with such slogans as "Kill A White A Day" and "One Settler – One Bullet."

One morning not long after I arrived in the city, I saw a prophetic tag on a downtown wall: "APLA – King William's Town – Queenstown – Grahamstown," a list of planned targets for APLA attacks. Soon after, in King William's Town, armed assailants stormed a private golf club reception, killing four; in Queenstown, APLA commandos waited for all black customers to exit the Queenstown Spur, a popular American-style eatery, before blowing the roof off the place, killing one and injuring dozens.

Because the Transkei was an "autonomous" territory within South Africa, "freedom fighters" from the Transkei would stage their attacks just outside its borders, targeting white farmers, the police and soldiers. After carrying out their missions, they would race back into the Transkei, taunting the South African Defence Force soldiers who were often in hot pursuit. One of the many ironies of this time in southern Africa was that the borders of the Transkei were, in fact, put in place by the architects of apartheid.

Our Pan African Congress contact in Queenstown, a church member named Chris Jabanga, would later talk about this with me, scratching his chin as he divulged what everyone in the intelligence community already knew – that these attacks by APLA guerrillas, reported in the media as "random hits," were anything but random. The targets were carefully selected and the attacks meticulously planned. And Umtata, where we were supposed to be doing missionary work, was at the heart of it all.

The Truth and Reconciliation Commission (TRC) would later officially describe APLA's activity this way:

The PAC proclaimed a military strategy of a "protracted people's war," which involved the infiltration of APLA guerrillas into the country to conduct rural guerrilla warfare. The initial targets of such attacks were members of the security forces and white farmers who were perceived to be the frontline of defence for the former apartheid government. A "repossession unit" was also set up, in which APLA cells conducted armed robberies on the instructions of the APLA High Command to raise funds and/or obtain weapons and vehicles to enable APLA to carry out its military strategy.

Hargraves and I would shake our heads in wonderment at the tags on the walls and the chalk outlines on the pavement and continue our runs to the far reaches of Southernwood, a high-end residential district that boasted newer and more elaborate homes than our older Norwood district. There we would meet up with Winston Dandala, who would occasionally join us on these early morning runs as the lot of us trained for an upcoming 5K "fun run."

The run, which was to be sponsored by the Transkei Development Authority, had been announced at our church meetinghouse, the Umtata Public Library, one particular Sunday, by the branch president, or local leader of our church, who wore a dapper, shiny tailored suit and announced the event three times, on account of his position as the public relations spokesperson for the Transkei Development Authority. I loved the dramatic effect of his announcements, repeated again and yet again.

"Brothers and sisters, we are going to have a 5K race, for charity," intoned Branch President Awuwa, going on to repeat himself in dramatic overtones, twice again, before continuing on. "And so, if you wish to take part, you must practice, practice, practice you must get off your backsides and run!"

And so we fell into a routine of working out with Winston, our good friend from Southernwood, who was middle-aged and liked to jog – which suited us elders just fine. Winston was "less active" so our runs together counted as missionary work, which I thought was funny, because it wasn't work at all – we all had such a good time together. I remember taking it easy, taking it slow, some youths of his neighborhood spotting us just starting out on our communal jog one morning near his house. They laughed, clicking their tongues in their native Xhosa, telling us we were running like old nannies and didn't have a chance in hell of winning the upcoming Transkei Authority Race. And we laughed right back, because for us it wasn't about speed or about a ribbon. It was about the experience, and the company.

But these runs with Winston also had a serious side. Winston worked for the ANC and he would tell us as we jogged along about the inner workings of what was then the major opposition party to the apartheid government. He was also our canary in the coalmine, keeping us apprised of the mood in the city and when it might be best for us to lay low at our house.

* * *

About this time, Hargraves and I were tracting a new development of homes in Umtata's Hillcrest district. Tracting consisted of knocking on doors, hoping the residents were home. We would usually find someone – a wife, a child or a husband – at which point we'd launch into a conversation about anything but religion. We'd talk about the weather while wiping our brows – *Shushu*, it's too hot; or about the flowers in the family garden – *Aren't they just wonderful?*; or about the neighborhood. We'd ask about the children's accomplishments, the husband's work, and eventually, quite shamelessly, steer the conversation toward *Thixo*, our God.

Thinking back now, it all sounds artificial and devious. But at that time, I thought of it simply as a way to meet and connect with people, to learn about their culture, to spread some good will in a strange land where we were trying to fit in. We were mandated, unfortunately, to inject religion into the conversations, but we would quickly move on to more general themes and offer to help in any way we could.

In such a low-key way, we met a "golden contact" family during a late-afternoon tracting session. The Mehlomakhulus were keen to learn what we were about and accepted our invitation to listen to the first discussion on the LDS faith. The Mehlomakhulu family was comprised of a father, mother and three or four small children, all extremely affable and gregarious. We shook everyone's hand and they smiled and invited us into their home. Inside, the baby of the family reached out to touch my hair, apparently never having seen a white, blond person. The baby oohed and aahed and then slapped me across the face, because I was different. But then he reached out and again stroked my hair, beginning to giggle. And we all broke into laughter.

By the time we'd finished telling them about God and Jesus and Joseph Smith, they had already signed up for the next discussion. The lot of us had hit if off famously and we were mutually eager to meet again soon.

When we made such a promising contact, like this one with the Mehlomakhulus, it was imperative to designate a church member in the local community to maintain the relationship with the prospective converts after the missionaries who first met them had long since flown home. So during one of our early morning runs with Winston, we asked if he would feel comfortable going with us to our second discussion with the Mehlomakhulus, to help answer any questions, to translate if necessary, to be their friend. "Sure, just tell me when to meet you," he said.

"Later this very night."

We swung around in our car, and picked Winston up, and took the drive together across the city and into the Hillcrest neighborhood, where the Mehlomakhulus resided, where we found Mr. Mehlomakhulu waiting for us on the front stoop of his home.

We parked and exited our car and as we smiled and laughed and slapped our friend Winston on the back, making our way up to the Mehlomakhulu house, I could see that something was wrong as the lights of the house were out and Mr. Mehlomakhulu had a blank look on his face, so very different from the last time we'd had the pleasure to meet.

"Brother Mehlomakhulu, how are you?" I called out as we approached. "What's up with the lights? Where's the family? How are you keeping?"

To which greetings Mr. Mehlomakhulu responded in a subdued voice, bringing his hands down in front of him several times to encourage us to follow suit, to lower our voices and not be so damned gleeful.

"You can never come back here, elders," he said. "I'm so sorry, but you can never come back."

We looked to Winston to see if there might have been some miscommunication, although Mr. Mehlomakhulu was speaking in fluent English. Winston shrugged his shoulders, indicating that he likewise didn't understand what was going on.

"Don't look, but the house directly across the street – it's an APLA base," Mr. Mehlomakhulu said. "It's an APLA safe house. You knocked on their door the same day you knocked on mine. And they came to pay me a visit and to threaten me just after you left."

That afternoon's events raced through my mind. We had knocked on the Mehlomakhulus' door and, after meeting with them, we canvassed the whole street, which ended in a cul-de-sac. I recalled knocking on the door of the APLA house across the street from the Mehlomakhulus. I was quite certain that people were in the house, just behind the door and the white sheet that formed a makeshift curtain for the front window. No one had answered, so I knocked again. I had had a strange feeling at the time, and now Mr. Mehlomakhulu's information about the house made the hairs on the back of my neck stand straight up.

"You can never come back, because if you do, they will kill me and they will kill my family," Mr. Mehlomakhulu said with fear in his voice. I felt sick at the thought that we wouldn't see him again, at least not here. No way would we put him and his family in danger. But I felt a connection with this family and wanted to stay in touch. Speaking just loud enough to be heard, I said, "I know we can no longer come to you, I understand that. But in time, when you're ready, if you feel safe about it, you can come to us. We meet at the Umtata Public Library at 10:45 on Sunday mornings. And you'd be more than welcome."

Mr. Mehlomakhulu shook his head in exasperation.

"No, you don't understand," he said. "They know everything. They know who you are. They know where you meet. They know where you come from. They know your names."

A group of *settlers* – a pejorative term for whites – representing an American-based religion, actively recruiting what, in their minds, would be considered *settler sympathizers*, meeting in a public space. Of course the local APLA knew all about us.

We wanted to shake hands, but no hand was offered. So we swallowed hard, nodded our heads and walked back to our car, taking one look back to the porch of our friend Mr. Mehlomakhulu. He stood there, a solitary figure in the dark, watching us go.

Back in the Corolla, Winston said, "OK, I want to see this house, I want to get a good look. I can tell you straightaway if they're serious or if these people are joking."

We made a U-turn at the cul-de-sac and drove back along the street. We slowed down so Winston could get a good look at the suspect house. As he peered through the car's back window, he abruptly ducked down and said in a harsh whisper, "Go, go, go! They're at the window. They're watching. This is bad, this is very, very bad! I tell you, that house isn't at all right!"

The look of terror on Winston's face spoke louder than his words. He was well acquainted with Umtata's various political organizations – their ideologies, their alliances, their rivalries, and which posed the most danger, particularly for whites. One good look and he knew that this *was* an APLA base. And behind that sheet in the window was a group of trained fighters whose mission was to kill settlers, to kill whites and to intimidate all who associated with them. We never again knocked on a door in the Hillcrest district of Umtata.

* * *

Hargraves and I had been running every morning, many times with Winston, and we felt pretty damned fit. We persuaded the other pair of missionaries who lived in our house to do the 5K run as well, even though they hadn't trained at all. They quite happily slept until the required 6:30 a.m. wake-up time as my companion and I were out punishing ourselves every morning at first light. Adler from Idaho and Brown from Arizona were a good-natured, likable pair. Brown was of medium height with dark hair and a pudgy middle. He talked slowly, methodically, and with emotion. Adler was a bit more delicate, a teenager from the Idaho prairie who aspired to be a concert pianist. He was short and wiry and he sported a shock of red hair and often a huge smile. It took some convincing to get them out jogging, or even walking for five kilometers, in a fun run under the African sun.

On the day of the race, when we all showed up at the downtown offices of the Transkei Development Authority, we saw a group of runners just finishing the 5K. *What the hell*, we wondered. *What happened to the start time?* We were told that the organizers decided at the last minute to stage the 5K run first. Which meant that if we wanted to take part in the event, we'd have to do the 10K race.

I was all for it, but my fellow missionaries, decked out in running shorts and competition T-shirts, were reluctant. "Come on, it's for a good cause," Mrs. Dandala, Winston's wife, said by way of encouragement.

We took a look at the finishers of the 5K race children and mothers and a few elderly folks still straggling in, and then at the runners at the starting line for the 10K run. They were a different breed serious athletes who were running in place, doing hard-core stretches, psyching themselves up. It appeared that many had come from East Africa. We spotted a TV camera and a reporter in a shiny suit and realized that the 10K would be far more demanding than the 5K "fun run." But then we saw what looked like office workers, some with potbellies, also gathering at the 10K starting line. They were mimicking the athletes' pre-run rituals, and that bolstered our confidence. "Sure, why not," we said, and got ready to run.

The starting pistol was fired and we were off. The faster runners jostled for position at the front of the pack while we and the desk jockeys held back and tried to husband our energy. The run began in the center of downtown and zigzagged through the commercial district before eventually coming to a steep hill just outside of town. The hot sun was directly above us and the run up the hill began sapping our strength. We refused to walk, but our running at this stage was not much faster than a brisk stroll. It felt like we were never going to reach the top, but at the moment when we were about to give up, we saw the lead runners coming back down and passing us on the return leg. The leaders, proudly displaying the flag of Kenya on their shirts, were running barefoot. That amazed me because the midday sun made the pavement hot to the touch. There were cash prizes for the winners and little question about who would cash in. Hargraves and I pressed on, keeping pace with Winston, determined to make the halfway point with him. We finally reached the top of the hill and savored the pleasure of turning around and cruising back down, with a cooling breeze at our backs. I kept a lookout for the other two elders, hoping that they were still in the race.

An ambulance customarily follows the last runners, ready to scoop up any who collapse from exhaustion or the heat. But Elders Brown and Adler had somehow managed to position themselves behind the ambulance, slowly placing one foot ahead of the other with looks of undisguised pain.

I lost track of Hargraves at some point along the return leg, and Winston and I finished among the top one hundred, back in the heart of the city. A cameraman perched on a small crane in the city center, recording the leaders' final strides before the finish line, switched off the big camera just before we approached. A minute earlier and we would have been on TV. But it didn't matter. We had finished!

Mrs. Dandala was waiting for us with cool drinks and snacks. Winston and I took a breather in the shade of a colonial-era building, propping up the pillars lining the sidewalk, hands on our knees, trying to breathe again at an even pace. Hargraves and Brown in time made it to the finish line as other 10K runners struggled to the end in dribs and drabs.

An hour later, Adler was nowhere to be seen. I asked around, but Hargraves and Brown hadn't seen him either. Tired runners congregated in small groups as our church leader, the PR man for the Transkei Development Authority, handed out ribbons, certificates and prizes. As I was really getting worried about Adler, the ambulance pulled up just in front of the finish line. I took one look and thought the worst. But as the ambulance stopped, the back doors burst open and out jumped Adler, hands in the air like he'd just won the Olympics marathon, smiling big and breathing easily. In dramatic fashion and with exaggerated steps, Adler made the final few strides across the finish line – in record-setting last place.

TOYI-TOYI

CHAPTER TWELVE

The children at the Transkei State Hospital greeted us with huge smiles whenever we arrived there for our twice-weekly visits. Playful, boisterous and curious, they were like any other children, except that they were suffering from tuberculosis, lower respiratory infections, HIV-AIDS and other serious illnesses. They had been brought to Umtata from all over rural Transkei – from Coffee Bay, from Butterworth, from Qunu, Nelson Mandela's home village, just down the road.

Some of the kids would approach us on makeshift crutches. One had been wounded by a shotgun blast, the scars left by the pellets arrayed across his tiny back. He had been caught in the crossfire between warring parties, waifish collateral damage of mindless violence.

We'd pull up outside the children's ward of mortar and brick and corrugated iron on the hospital grounds, parking our battered Corolla under the shade of a sneeze-wood tree, and make our way forward, and it didn't take long before we were mobbed by hugs and by slaps on the back. The kids asking us how we had been, of how *we* were holding up.

As aid volunteers, it was our job to make these kids smile, to play games, to dance, to laugh, to sing, to forget their woes, if only for the afternoon. Say what you will about white missionaries in Africa, but looking back after all of these years, I can say that I loved this time of my life more than any other. Not because of our mandated mission to convert people to the LDS faith, but because of the opportunity to do some good in a troubled place.

An eye of one of the boys from the children's ward was swollen shut, apparently from some sort of infection, but his bright smile was more than enough to distract from his disfigurement. His friend, a kid about the same size and sporting a matching smile, would hold his hand and close one of his eyes when he was with him, in solidarity. A little girl who wore a pink plastic comb in her hair and carried a matching pink mirror wouldn't go anywhere without her fluffy white plush doll. I couldn't make out what kind of animal it was supposed to be, but she obviously loved it as she dragged it around the children's ward. The doll, the comb and the mirror must have been her only worldly possessions. The girl was shy and slow to smile, but when she did it was genuine and heartwarming, well worth the wait. All of these children were hard-luck kids, but they seemed to be thankful for what little they had. They had each other. And, for us, they always had smiles.

One game that we'd regularly play was called "Fire on the Mountain," in which the kids would run around in a circle, one of them calling out in English and then Xhosa: "There's a fire on the mountain! Run! Run! *Kukh'umlilo kwezantaba! Baleka! Baleka!*" The kids would whip themselves into a frenzy, racing around the circle until they heard the word "Statue!" At which point everyone would freeze, as if they'd been turned into stone. Those who twitched or laughed would have to leave the circle. The one who could freeze and remain motionless through multiple rounds was the winner.

It was all in fun, and only later did I realize that the game was a metaphor for the kids' fragile lives. All of these kids were in real danger, like a village of children living on the slope of an active volcano, who at any moment might be taken in mid stride by the volcano's eruption. For the children of Transkei State Hospital, the fire on the mountain was malnourishment and disease.

But for those moments in time, as they'd run around in circles, unable to control their emotions, positively giddy with joy, they were free. They screamed and they laughed, they jumped up in the air and they played. In so doing, their problems and their pain and the bum cards they'd been dealt in this life were pushed out of mind and out of sight. They were pushed clean away.

The kids had been practicing several weeks for a musical performance, to sing for us their favorite songs. On the appointed day, I came with a portable tape recorder. The kids were a bit nervous, but they soon warmed to the idea and gave it their all. The auntie of the ward offered words of encouragement, as did we. The children sang many songs, but their favorite was one called *Si sindisiwe ngegazi lika Yesu*, whose chorus in Xhosa translates as: "We rejoice! We are happy! We are content!"

I felt at peace when I listened to these children sing. I remember the kids' indifference to the fact that our skin was a different color, that I was white and they were black, that I was American and they were South African. It is true, we came from different worlds, but from the moment we'd pull up under the shade of that sneeze-wood tree and the kids would emerge from their ward, and we'd smile, we were one.

* * *

Late one night we went to visit with a member of our church, a mother who worked as a nurse at the Transkei State Hospital. We were keen to see her and her family because we liked them a great deal, but we were also eager to learn more about a strike that we heard was being planned at the hospital.

"The problem is we haven't been paid, for months," said the family matriarch, still wearing her white and maroon hospital uniform. She had poured us each a cup of rooibos bush tea and had taken a seat, cradling her own cup of tea in her hands, taking occasional sips as she talked of the impending work stoppage.

"We don't mind working," she said. "We like our jobs. We like to help people, but we also have to feed our own babies. *We* also have to eat."

As a professional, the woman had a comfortable home and was fairly well off. So her intention to strike seemed more about principle than an actual need to pay for food for her family.

As missionaries who helped at the hospital, we had been looking at the prospect of a strike from the patients' perspective. But now, hearing of the nurses' grievances, we gained a new understanding.

The hospital had been running on a deficit for some time and the Transkei government had been promising payment for months. So the problem wasn't really the owed back payment, considering that the hospital had survived until this point. The problem was that the nurses felt that if they didn't act now they might never be paid again.

We asked what would happen to the patients. I was struggling to keep up with the conversation because of our personal interest as hospital volunteers.

"Those that can leave, we've already started to send

home," the nurse said. "It's not the people we have a problem with, you understand. It's not the patients. It's this government. We've told them – and we mean it – if they don't pay up we're going to *toyi-toyi*. We're going to strike. We're going to close down that hospital until our demands are met and the government takes us seriously."

Toyi-toyi, a Xhosa warrior dance, frequently used in street demonstrations, in a broader context could mean any kind of protest, such as a boycott or a strike.

Hargraves and I for some time had been working just about all of our waking hours – going to meetings and church services, volunteering and tracting new areas. The workload had taken a toll on me and I took sick. I didn't want to acknowledge it because I didn't have time to be sick.

The nurse noticed my pallor and loss of weight, clucked her concern and suggested that I see a doctor. I agreed to go to a doctor the next day. Then, as an afterthought, she asked if I was allergic to any medications. I thought for a moment and said, "Yeah, as a matter of fact, I am. I'm allergic to penicillin."

We bade farewell, and for the rest of that night and into the next morning I took up residence in our bathroom, sick over the toilet bowl, on the verge of passing out from dehydration and exhaustion.

Hargraves made some phone calls and found a private doctor who would see me. He helped me to the car and drove me across town to the doctor's office.

The physician was a friendly Xhosa, who wore a suit and loose-fitting tie instead of a white lab coat. He had just come from his home, opening his practice on a Saturday to see me.

He asked where I was from and we exchanged pleasantries, even though I didn't feel very pleasant. I liked him immediately but was nervous at the prospect of getting an injection because I have a phobia about shots. As the doctor listened to my heart, checked out my ears and throat, tapped on my knees and did a battery of other tests, we talked about anything and everything but my health. I was steering the conversation to any and all irrelevant topics to avoid thinking about the possibility of a long, sharp needle piercing my skin.

The doctor picked up on my aversion to injections. He chuckled and patted me on the back as he delivered the dreaded news that, yes, I did need a shot. He told me to go next door to another examining room where his nurse would administer the injection.

Weakling that I was, I sheepishly went next door and rolled up my sleeve as the nurse came in. She was a bruiser of a woman, heavy on her feet and all business. She didn't say a word as she readied the needle, which seemed bigger than usual on account of my terror at its sight. As I watched in trepidation, she tapped the syringe a couple of times until a drop of liquid leaked out of the business end of the needle. She placed the tip of the needle against my bare arm, now covered with goose bumps, and hesitated a moment before thrusting it into my bloodstream. That moment seemed to take longer than it should, and as I sat there and watched the needle deliberate, a saving grace of a thought came to my mind, and I verbalized it. "Stop!" I said. "I'm allergic to penicillin! What is in that needle? Does it contain a taste of penicillin?"

In the United States, nurses almost always ask a patient about any allergies before being seen by the doctor. They record your weight, your height, your blood pressure, and ask if you're allergic to anything. But in Africa, it's up to the patient to raise the matter. If our nurse friend had not asked me the night before, I would never have remembered my allergic reaction to penicillin as a child. I hadn't thought about it for years, and now I was so weak and my mind so addled that I certainly wouldn't have remembered it save for the previous night's conversation. But with the needle poised on my arm, my mind screamed *Danger!* I asked the question more to avoid the pain of the injection than to save my life. And at the last moment, the nurse flinched and pulled the needle away. "No, child," she said, "this shot doesn't contain a *taste* of penicillin. It is pure penicillin!"

I rolled down my sleeve and marched back into the doctor's main room, where I told him of what had happened when I was a small child.

"I'd had strep throat when I was about five years old and went to the hospital with my mom in Los Angeles," I said. "The doctors gave me a shot that released more and more penicillin into my system every day. They didn't know that I was deathly allergic, and once they realized it, they thought it was going to kill me.

"They put me in one of those see-through plastic tents that they put premature babies into, to monitor them," I continued. "They thought I was a goner, but for some reason I survived. They told my mom to tell me that if I ever had even the slightest taste of penicillin as an adult, it'd kill me."

I asked this Xhosa doctor what would have happened, if his nurse had administered the injection. He was now deadly serious.

"*Yhuuu!*" he said, thinking for a moment before offering his professional opinion. "First, you would have gone into shock and then your body would have gone into spasmodic convulsions. Then, your lungs would have collapsed. Then, you would have started flopping all about the examination room like a fish out of water – gasping for air – but there would have been none. And then you would have died. And there would have been nothing I could have done to save you."

"*Yhuuu!*" I said, whistling through my teeth. "That wouldn't have been a very good way to go, would it?"

"*No*, it wouldn't," the doctor replied.

* * *

I recovered quickly and in a few days was back on my feet. It struck me as unfair that — because I was an American and had money to pay — I had access to a doctor who would open his office on a Saturday, while, for an ordinary Xhosa patient, seeing a doctor on a weekend would have been much harder, or impossible. But it was what it was.

An even greater unfairness was what was happening at the Transkei State Hospital — the government not paying the nurses, the nurses planning to strike, patients being sent home as a result, and others left without care. We worried about the remaining patients, those who had no homes to go to and no one to care for them.

Rule No. 110: Provide community service.
Rule No. 111: Do not provide community service
that isn't approved by your mission president.
Rule No. 112: Do not provide more than four hours
a week of community service.

The nurses did go on strike as promised. After a few days of their work stoppage, we made a few phone calls to find out if we could still visit the kids and help care for them. One of our calls was to the hospital, where a doctor finally answered the phone. He told us that the situation was dire, that the doctors were the only care-givers still at the hospital and that they were hard-pressed just to provide the most basic of services — getting food to the patients. "There are patients who are going to starve if we can't feed them," the doctor said.

As district leader of the LDS missionaries in Umtata, I made phone calls up the chain of command. I spoke first to our leaders in Queenstown and then to the mission office in Cape Town, where the assistants to the president handed the phone to President Bingham.

I told him of our work with the children at the hospital. I told him that the nurses were on strike and blocking the entrance, that the doctors were pleading for help in just feeding the remaining patients, and that some of them might die. I asked for permission to suspend our proselytizing, muster all of the Umtata-based missionaries to cross the picket line and volunteer at the hospital full time until the strike ended. I feared that he would say no – that above and beyond our allotted four hours per week of community service, we needed to be out knocking on doors. But, to my surprise, he said, "Yes, Elder Moore. Do what you have to do. Break that line and stay there and help the doctors with whatever they need you to do, for as many days as it takes."

The four of us elders who were based in Umtata drove to the hospital and parked just across the street from the main gate to the hospital grounds.

The nurses were out in full force, jumping up and down, shaking their placards all about, dancing and jiving and blocking the front entrance with their presence and with their weight and with their determination.

It wasn't going to be easy to get through, but get through we must. I thought of the kids inside and the thought of them made me angry, and I gunned the engine from across the street, our car jerking to life as it made a beeline for the gate. The nurses scrambled to block us, but we came straight for them, only slowing, and skidding to a sudden stop just before we hit them.

They rocked the car back and forth and put their placards up to the windows so we could read them. With the transmission in neutral, I gunned the engine again and then shifted into first gear and nudged the car forward, ever so slowly. The noise of the revving engine was no match for the chants and shouts of the striking nurses. Seeing that we were determined to pass through the gate, they finally moved aside to let us in.

What we saw inside of that hospital is a blur in my memory, to this very day, because it was just too awful. The few doctors on site were scrambling. And the hospital was nearly deserted – patients having been released, having been sent packing, having been sent home, all patients who were not terminal, who were not in danger of losing their lives. But as the hospital was so big there were still lots of people.

We helped the doctors with getting water to patients and with the food for some time, running plates from ward to ward, a cook stewing up a big pot of mealie meal, a corn-based porridge, clear over on the other end of the hospital, from where we were used to visiting.

One of the international doctors from Europe, who was young and doing his residency here in the Transkei, showed us a medical cabinet that'd been padlocked up, the nurses having taken away the keys. He said that this was the problem – that the doctors were useless without their nurses because they, as doctors, simply diagnosed and prescribed. That they wrote the scripts for the drugs but that a lot of the time they didn't even know what the drug bottles looked like. That it was the nurses who in reality controlled the place and wielded the power because they knew the patients and they knew the drugs. That the patients needed medicine – that without the medicine and without the nurses to administer it, the situation was hopeless. That the drugs that had not been locked away into the cupboards had been spirited away by the nurses. So they would be needed. So they would be missed. So the nurses' demands would be met.

The hospital was a sprawling complex of out-buildings and after helping for quite some time where we were being directed to help, in time we broke away and made our way on foot to the children's ward, to Ward Number Six, where instead of being met by a group of bright and cheerful faces, we found only a handful of children in their hospital beds, barely hanging on.

I don't remember this part of the story clearly because I've blocked it out for all these years. I don't remember if I went to the children's ward by myself or with other missionaries. What I do remember is that the children, whom we knew by name, were in serious trouble because they weren't getting their life-saving medicine.

As I ran from bed to bed to rustle the kids, to try to get them to respond, to attempt to encourage them on to a smile, I remember looking for the worst of the lot, and that it hadn't taken me long to find him. His name was Asanda, and he came from the intensely beautiful Wild Coast village of Coffee Bay. He'd been one of the more animated of the lot on visits past, from the moment we'd swoop in for a visit, forever refusing to let my hand go. The little boy's smile had been infectious. You never would have believed that he was sick in the past, for he'd encourage his playmates on, chanting and laughing and smiling. But now he was sprawled out on his bed and he refused to respond – to my presence or to my nudging, or to my taking his little hand in my own. He wasn't moaning or responding in any way whatsoever and yet the expression on his face looked as if he were in pain. My only thought was to get him to that international resident doctor, that if I could locate the doctor, any doctor, it would all be okay, that Asanda would be okay. Without thinking, I grabbed him out of his bed and ran with him through the hallway, and out into the light, onto the dirt path that connected the various buildings, screaming, yelling for somebody, for anybody to help. This once-lively sprite of a boy I had played with and had sung with and had danced with was dying. Right there in my arms. I ran and I ran as fast as my legs would carry me, but there was nobody to help us, there was nobody who answered my call for help.

I cry when I think of it now, when I put pen to paper all these years later, when I stop for a moment to contemplate and to let that most horrid of all memories back in. That the inevitable might be true, that the inevitable was indeed true. That the little child's body had become a rigid burden in my arms. That we had lost him. That Asanda was gone.

EPILOGUE

The township Mdantsane was insanely colorful, especially on *NgeCawe*, or Sunday, women strutting to and from their various churches in intensely vivid gowns, called *ooMama beBhatyi*, meaning women's jackets, emblematic of their various church societies. Purple was for Anglicans, red for Methodists, and blue for the Zion Christian Church, whose members also wore green and black ribbons with shiny Stars of David. The Zionists were so proud of their emblem that they wore it every day of the week.

Out on foot one day in one of the more rough and tumble zones of the township, we met up with a representative of the Zion Christian Church. The kid was named Simphiwe and he was decked out in a khaki safari suit, just like mine, save for his bright white shoes, what looked like a big black train conductor's hat and a bright silver star embossed with the letters ZCC pinned to his suit's lapel. He introduced himself as an *umfundisi* and looked to be just about our age, but in reality he was a bit older, already the bishop, or leader, of his congregation.

The ZCC is South Africa's largest African-initiated church,

and we had a lot of respect for it. Its members were readily identified by their badges and known for their humility. Another mark of the denomination was the sheer energy that ZCC members put into their worship services: clapping, jumping, beating of drums and the singing of African-based songs (as opposed to Western hymns), which one could usually hear a right fur piece down the road.

From the start, we took a shine to Simphiwe. We would often swing by his home in Zone 1 to talk shop, to exchange stories about our respective congregants, to talk about life in the township and to share our hopes and dreams.

I liked the young leader's smile and his outlook on life, his outlook on the world, not seen through the rose-tinted lens of the "saved" but as a realist, a dreamer, and a leader. Simphiwe wanted us to understand a bit about his world, about how his flock lived, of how they struggled, of how they survived.

He invited us to visit his church. "Come on, *umfundisi*," he said. "You're here in Africa, so you should come and witness an African church, a church of Africa in action."

With that smile he could ask for and receive anything he wanted, and we responded: "Absolutely, yes."

So one Sunday Simphiwe took us to his church and introduced us with great fanfare to a portion of his flock, dressed in their Sabbath uniforms and already riled up with the spirit of the Lord. The women were dressed in blue and the men in khaki safari jackets, all of them stomping and clapping, the drums keeping rhythm as the choir sang in perfect harmony. Simphiwe let us take a turn at the drums, which was awesome. He later took us to the home of a sickly old lady who was too weak to attend services. In the dim light of her bedroom we could just make out her form as she looked up from her bed as we entered. The wick of the bedside lamp was lit and the room smelled of kerosene as she struggled to sit up in bed to see us. We each shook her hands, which were weak and yet feisty, clinging on to life, much like my mother's just before I departed my own home, I noted. The woman's smile was strained but it was wise and oh so beautiful, and as she smiled, that smile in my own mind's eye morphed into my mother's. It was a smile of love and of humility. It was the wizened old smile of a life well lived. We told her, in Xhosa, how nice it was to meet her, and she returned the favor and stated that no, that it was nicer for her to meet us. At long last, we exited and made our way, with our friend, Simphiwe, up and onto a little hill near his home that housed an abandoned elementary school.

We were trailed by kids everywhere we went with our new friend, the children rolling abandoned tires and homemade wire toy cars with sticks along our path, the braver of the lot laughing and holding our hands, swinging our arms as we walked, as we were guided about.

The ruins of the school atop the hill were a testament to the gross inequity of South Africa's apartheid system. One look around and we could see why it had been shunned and abandoned. Besides the pages of books in Afrikaans strewn about the site, the building itself was dismal, dreary and completely lacking in any enticements for young kids. Long, squat and purely utilitarian, it was built of cinder blocks like the homes in the township. Its windows were shattered, shards of glass littered the dry, cracked ground and its doors hung askew on rusty broken hinges. The school had no electricity. Its interior light came from kerosene lanterns, now coated with dust as they hung from hooks in the ceiling. The inside of the structure was as hot as a furnace, even with all the doors and windows wide open. In such conditions, the chances of these children making it in the wider world were doomed from the start.

As we emerged into a fresh breeze and the glorious light of midday, Simphiwe looked to us to see if we understood. We nodded in the affirmative. There was no need for words. I saw in his face, as in the faces of others in the township, the same stoic determination. They would not let this system define them. Things had to change.

* * *

The membership of our church had been commuting out to East London for worship services, which was a hell of a schlep. So it came as a godsend to open up shop in the location proper, to find a spot to meet at the NU 7 community centre right smack in the middle of the township. I'd often thought how wrong it was that the people with the least had been expected to find their way to East London and back each Sunday, in fair weather and foul. But now they had their own meetinghouse. The building was modern and multi-purpose, the ceiling high and the walls comprised of glass partitions, which could be opened up in the summer months. We gave the locals assignments to come early and unlock the building and to set up the chairs and to greet people at the front doors.

Brother Robenheimer, the white leader of the Mormon Church in East London, brought his young family to our first service. In his remarks to the small congregation, he predicted that this is where the church would see the most growth, that he could envision hundreds, perhaps thousands, of followers in the not-too-distant future, right here in Mdantsane.

We looked about to the fifteen or so folks gathered that day and scratched our heads and then from out of nowhere, just after we'd kicked ourselves into the opening stanza of one of our American-based church hymns, there came a tapping on the window and we looked up and witnessed several hundred Xhosas at the wall of a window. Still others were approaching, their footfalls stirring up a dusty haze in the vacant lot next to the community center.

Everybody's first reflex reaction was trouble; that we were quite possibly under attack. The Robenheimers gasped, followed by a glare of concern from all within the walls of our centre. I didn't know what to make of the crowd's presence until I saw their ribbons and their stars and knew they were here in friendship. I scanned the oncoming multitude and spotted Simphiwe, his smile ever-present, quite literally beaming that bright Sunday morning in simile with the sun.

I ran back to the main doors at the front of the building and called out to welcome him and he shook my hands, African-style, telling me, "It's only fair, Elder Moore. You came to visit our church and so the lot of us decided we would return the favor and come and visit yours."

The moment was brilliant. It was nothing short of brilliant. And it made me smile, because everybody just outside our makeshift church was smiling, and as I announced to our church members that we had some visitors, they began to laugh, and the tension broke, just like that. They immediately got up and began to unfold as many chairs as they could find as the entire membership of the Zion Christian Church came streaming in, black and green ribbons and golden stars shining, shaking our hands as they entered. They had traveled by foot, half the township away, all the way from Zone 1.

* * *

Simphiwe bent our ear a few days later to ask a favor, as he put it. To which we replied, "Sure, anything." We were halfway through an afternoon lunch at the young bishop's home, dining with him over a traditional meal of *umphokoqo* – mealie meal with sour milk – when he told us the old woman whom we'd been to visit together a few weeks back had succumbed to old age and had passed. He wanted us to attend the funeral, and asked me to give a speech.

"She was a very old lady," he told us. "And she was happy to meet you. You were the only *mlungus* to ever visit her – and you did her heart good."

Mlungu is a Xhosa word widely used to describe white people. It literally means "white sea foam," which really is rather appropriate. For the sickly-pale, off-white sea foam washes up along the coastline of Southern Africa, just as the Europeans had done.

We went to the old woman's home the following day to pay our respects, and found the preparations for her funeral in full swing. Her body was in a casket just outside the back door, the house was packed wall to wall with family and guests and the choir was already wailing. Although we tried to decline, two chairs were made available for us in the home's front room, where we sat across a makeshift table from an older African man in an old-fashioned suit and a plaid bow tie. He declined to shake hands, introducing himself as "Dr." somebody.

"I'm not a medical doctor," he said. "You see, the title 'Dr.' is on account of my Ph.D. in philosophy." The man told us that if we wished to address him we should call him "Doctor," like everyone else. So we called him "Doctor," and his gruff demeanor softened, if only just a bit.

"I studied in Europe," the man said with a dismissive gesture, as if that was nothing. "But I decided to return. To come back to South Africa, but not only South Africa, to come back to the township, to where I am from.

"My plane landed in Cape Town and the police boarded it before my fellow passengers and I could disembark," he said. "They demanded to see my papers and I thought, 'What have I done?' For I was the only black man on the aircraft, and I didn't have to come back. And I answered my own question with one simple phrase: 'I have come home.'

"You see, I can live in the city if I want to, I can live in East London, but I'm living here, right in the township, to make a point," the man told us. "That I can live anywhere I want to live that no white man can tell me any longer what is what."

We knew a bit about South Africa's pass laws and the history of the Group Areas Act. We told him that we wholeheartedly agreed with him and that we also had chosen to live inside Mdantsane. The gent broke into an epic smile and chuckled. He called us "true liberals" and shook our hands. We then got on just fine.

The funeral cortege of hired buses passed out of the township and into the countryside of rural Ciskei, amid rolling green hills, far off the beaten track. The procession descended into a shallow valley to a cluster of *rondovals*, round huts made of mud and thatch, and the buses parked beside a large thorn tree. The casket had been transported ahead and it now sat open inside one of the *rondovals*, where relatives and members of the Zion Christian Church passed by the corpse wailing their grief and saying their final farewells.

Outside, a fire was readied to roast several goats that were brought forward and ceremoniously slaughtered at Simphiwe's direction. As the goats' throats were cut, they crumpled to the ground, their front legs bending down as if in supplication, as if in prayer.

The goats were skinned and gutted and put on long spits over the fire as chairs were set up on the red sandy ground. Much sooner than I'd expected the goats were deemed ready, and we were encouraged to partake of the hunks of roasted meat. In rural South Africa, when a person dies, it is the responsibility of the family to feed the entire village.

I took my seat behind the makeshift podium and surveyed the scene, trying to conjure this old woman's childhood. I imagined her playing with siblings and friends on this very patch of ground. But I didn't know at the time that the family was not originally from these parts at all. In the 1940s, I learned later in the afternoon from a succession of eulogies, that the woman and her family had been "repatriated" to their "homeland" from a more bountiful region of South Africa preferred by whites.

What I likewise didn't know was that gatherings of any sort by Bantus were banned by the National Party regime – except at funeral services, far out in the hinterlands, just like the one we were attending on this torrid, late-summer afternoon.

A couple hundred chairs were set out for the mourners and about ten for those making speeches. About half of the men who spoke that day began their remarks with a raised clenched fist and the rallying cry *Amandla!* ("Power!"). To which about half of the audience would stand and respond, *Ngawhethu!!* ("To the people!").

The speakers said little about the lady who had died and a whole lot about the political situation in South Africa. They spoke of recent police raids in Mdantsane, the general plight of the majority blacks and what had to be done to turn things about. The overall message was: We need to be unified and we need to stand strong.

There was talk of boycotts of white-owned businesses, blocking the road between Mdantsane and East London and the relative merits of the African National Congress and the rival Pan African Congress, which took a harder line against the whites. It was easy to see which party each speaker represented, and each elicited passionate responses from backers in the audience. By my estimate, each of the political parties had about an equal number of followers among the spectators.

When it was my turn to speak, there was a hush in the crowd as I stood up. Every sentence I spoke was translated into Xhosa, except for my halting opening remarks in their language. I said that I was honored to take part in this occasion and that my name was Siyabonga, which prompted applause and laughter.

Shifting to English, I told the people that I was their brother, that I will always remember the bright smile of the woman who had died, that I was impressed by her tenacious hold on life until the end and that I was a better person for having met her.

I gazed out at the horizon, a seemingly endless succession of rolling green hills, and back to the faces of the people gathered that day, to the members of the choir swaying gently in song, to the doctor of philosophy, clasping his hands and listening intently, and finally to Simphiwe, whose smile radiated love and compassion.

In the heat of that afternoon, I found it hard to speak as I closed my eyes and tried to concentrate on the woman we were gathered to honor. My mind drifted to the countless others who had parted from this life, and particularly to those whom I had known and loved – my brother, my mother, the boy from the hospital, this old woman. They were now cherished memories. But instead of sadness, their memory, their courage and their example gave me hope. I stood there transfixed, enveloped in the love of all those who had gone before and of those still here, who had embraced

a stranger trying to find his way in an alien land.

ACKNOWLEDGEMENTS

I am grateful to my dear friend Joanne Wiehahn Smith for her advice, assistance and support. To my editor and friend, James R. Peipert, for his patience, wisdom and passion for all things Africa. *Ndibulela kakhulu u* Pumza Sixishe for editing my rusty Xhosa, and for her love and sisterhood from day one, many moons ago. Thanks to my former missionary/aid-worker compadres and companions — in particular to Kilbs, Parkin, Brown, Drake, Gaudette, Stamps, Young and the Wrights. To Kurt Multhaup, Steve Cypert, Ben Peipert, Syd Goldsmith, James Spencer, Patty Rijo, Cameron Blake, Carole Nichols, Brenda Scarratt, David Smith and Nick Cummings, for their unwavering inspiritment. To the wit and beauty of Zarina Rose Lagman and her unique book designs. Cheers to Kai and Robert Easton for use of their lovely Long Street, Cape Town digs, *Chez Lulu*, where I found my voice and began work on this narrative. And lastly, I'd like to thank my personal heroes, Wynette Jameson and Kathy Eldon, for their smiles, encouragement and for conjuring the legacy of Dan and his mantra, *The journey is the destination.*

Neal Moore is the co-author of *Down the Mississippi* (Mark Twain Museum Press). A nomad, adventurer and storyteller, Neal's reporting has taken him from night-market meetings with Chinese cyber-dissidents to mountaintop encounters with approaching super typhoons. His work from North America, Africa and the Far East has appeared in *Der Spiegel*, *The New Yorker* and on CNN International.

He currently divides his time between Taipei, Cape Town and Addis Ababa.

CPSIA information can be obtained
at www.ICGtesting.com
Printed in the USA
LVOW11s1005201217
560207LV00063B/33/P